legacy

legacy

*A Step-by-Step Guide to
Writing Personal History*

Linda Spence

Swallow Press / Ohio University Press
Athens

Swallow Press/Ohio University Press, Athens, Ohio 45701
© 1997 Linda Spence
Printed in the United States of America
All rights reserved. Published 1997

Swallow Press/Ohio University Press books are printed on acid-free paper ∞ ™

01 00 99   9 8 7

Library of Congress Cataloging-in-Publication Data
Spence, Linda.
    Legacy : a step-by-step guide to writing personal history / by Linda Spence.
    p. cm.
    ISBN 0-8040-1002-1 (alk. paper). — ISBN 0-8040-1003-X (pbk. : alk. paper)
    1. Autobiography—Authorship. 2. Report writing. I. Title.
  CT25.C62 1997
  808'.06609—dc21

                       97-23680
                        CIP

The following people kindly donated photographs from their personal collections. Permission to reproduce these photographs is gratefully acknowledged: Chiquita Babb, Gillian Berchowitz, the Daijogo family, Helen Gawthrop, Richard Gilbert, Donna Kalis, Cliff McCarthy, Bonnie Rand, David Sanders, Linda Spence, Janalee Stock, Stan Swanson, Tanya Thompson, and Judy Wilson.

Contents

Preface

A few summers ago, my two sisters and I spent three weeks driving across the country, taking routes similar to ones we had taken as a family forty years ago. We visited our father's hometown, a place we hadn't seen for all those years. Sitting on a step of the front porch of a slightly shabby house divided into apartments, we took a picture mimicking the one our father had taken of us, when it was our grandparents' wide verandah with the rocking chairs and cool green ferns. Basking there in the warm southern sun, I felt another kind of warmth as we stared out at the front lawn and brought back memories of the dusk games of Kick the Can that our father organized, the fireflies just out of reach, and the comfort of familiar grown-up voices drifting up the stairs as we lay in our beds hoping for a cool breeze. On that trip we compared notes on how we remembered what we had done together as a family, and we offered each other what we knew of our parents' early years. Other than where they had lived and gone to school, we knew very little. This didn't surprise me as I have clear memories of myself as a child hanging around the kitchen or leaning over the front seat of the car, badgering them with questions about their lives. Somehow the subject always was dropped as the frosting bowl needed to be scraped or another road-song was begun.

By the time my sisters and I made that nostalgic summer trip, our parents were no longer living, and *Legacy* was close to completion. I had been moved to begin work on *Legacy* by my mother and my sister.

I was encouraged to stay with the project by people's eager responses—their dreamy look and earnest, "Ohhh, I wish I had a copy of that for my . . ." then they'd name a relative or someone close. Often I'd hear, "I might start one myself."

My daughter keeps saying, "I hope you're writing your Legacy." I am. So I have an idea of what lies ahead for you, and I warmly welcome you and encourage you to begin.

The Gift of Legacy

This book is a gift—a gift of hope, of commitment to life and loved ones, a gift of affection. To give it to someone to use or to use it yourself is to share with others these gifts of hope, commitment, and love.

Legacy is about life. About the times we've lived in, the people and events that have helped shape us, how and whom we've loved, what has stirred us, and how we've tried. When there's been laughter and when the tears have come—those times are here, too.

What goes into living a life during your time, in your particular place? This is what our children want to know. This is what we share with our dearest friends. It's an affirmation of the familiar phrase, "We're all in this together," something we seem to sense when we're very young, yet understand more deeply as we have time to reflect on our lives. Take the time. Tell us. Acknowledge the *together* of today and tomorrow, by giving your stories. The story of a life is a priceless legacy.

Whether you are using this guide yourself or giving it as a gift, the primary purpose of *Legacy* is to help reveal and preserve, easily and comfortably, the essence of one's life. If you suspect the recipient of your gift may need encouragement to begin, there are several ways you can help. Starting with "Why Write," read the introductory sections together. Express what it would mean to you to have a completed Legacy book. Your desire to know her or his life better may be the key incentive the writer needs to get started. The Legacy writer will need a book to write in—refer to the "Practice of Writing" section for suggestions. Whatever you choose, keep it simple. It's important that the book becomes theirs and that they are comfortable writing in it. As my sister said to me, "You know we'd have been thrilled if Mother or Dad had handed us a stack of dog-eared composition books filled with their stories." A smooth writing pen, a mug full of well-sharpened pencils, and your words of interest and encouragement would complete the gift.

Check in on the Legacy writer occasionally: How is it going? Who have you remembered that you hadn't thought of for a long time? What have you found yourself thinking about?

If the recipient of your gift is unable to do the actual writing, use the *Legacy* questions as springboards for conversation, or take down the words yourself. If she or he is comfortable having the responses mechanically recorded, a video or audio tape would be fine as an added dimension, but a transcribed copy on paper in an attractive binder would be a more lasting and accessible record to pass on to following generations. If there is an initial hesitancy, here's where you read aloud "Why Write?" and "Hesitating?" Then look through the questions for something you know they'll feel comfortable talking about and just listen. A few times together like this will assure your interest, and after a while you'll find the memories come easily. (This works long distance on the telephone, if necessary.) Remember that it's important to *listen* and that silences are a part of remembering and revisiting long-forgotten memories.

In many communities, schools have initiated community-wide oral history programs. The *Legacy* guide is an invaluable tool for these programs, providing a framework for the process of recording oral histories as well as specific questions to ask, building the confidence of a new generation of community historians and writers.

Legacy is a gift you want fully used and worn, so do what you can to nurture the process. You will be forever grateful for the part you play.

Why Write?

One day years ago, I found my usually contented mother in a curious state. She was seated, with a book in her lap, looking wistfully, somewhat mournfully, out the window. She held up the book, a recent gift from my sister, showed me its clean, white blank pages. "Your sister wants me to write about my life. I'd like to do it for her. . . ." Here, she trailed off, shook her head doubtfully, ". . . *but what does she want to know?*"

What indeed? What is that precious gift we ask of our elders? Scores of people, young and old, hearing of my work with *Legacy*, have volunteered their answers. A teenager wants to know, did her grandmother love music, did she dance, and to what music? A young sports enthusiast wonders, what games did grandfather play? A beginning cook longs for his mother's recipes, and wonders if mother remembers any of grandmother's recipes, or, better yet, wrote them down?

We are surprisingly curious about these everyday details. And many of us long for something more, something deeper: "I wanted to know," my sister tells me, "not just what happened in Mother's life, *but what she felt when it was happening.*"

We who have already lost our opportunity say, "I wish I'd known him better" or "I wish I could go back and ask her about that." Frequently, we hear "All I have left are a few family photographs." We stare at the face in the faded photograph, try to imagine the heart, the feelings, the story of that person. We pass on what stories we know, telling and retelling, drawing from them a sense of family identity and continuity.

Many of us are separated from our families by distance and busy lives. Few of us have the good fortune to spend long afternoons together—playing cards, listening to music, baking bread, sitting on the porch, and hearing the casual or intimate tales of "back then." Rarely do we work side by side with our parents, witnessing how they deal with life's surprises and challenges. Less and less frequently are our dinner tables set for several generations coming together to share a meal and the day's events. Even as our telephones bring us together in an instant, it is at the expense of letters, the written record of everyday life.

It is the everyday joys and sorrows as well as the "big events" that provide the fertile connecting ground between generations. And today, as we realize our losses, few of us find the journal or stack of letters that might have helped us to piece together the insight or real life story we seek. "What does—did—Mother remember of that summer; what was it like for her?" Madeleine L'Engle asks in *Summer of the Great-Grandmother*; "I don't even know why we were there, without Father, and it is too late to ask her. I can only remember the summer as it was for me, not as it was for her."

This is a book waiting to become your story. Parts of your life may already be known to others, but don't assume that what seems obvious to you will be familiar to them; and here, too, are questions that may not yet have been asked. If no one has asked, someone someday will, and this written record could be their only chance to get your answers. In *Legacy* you are invited to share your experiences, insights, and the wisdom and humility of your years.

Finally, the gift you give to others will repay you many times over and could become the gateway to a wider vision of your life. Your reflections and responses can uncover a purpose you may not have known or realized, a resolution and awareness of your life's fullness. So *Legacy* is for you and for all of us, writers and readers alike, honoring our lives, our stories, and our times.

Hesitating?

Maybe you're ready to dive right in and begin writing. If so, skip this section and move ahead to "How to Read *Legacy*."

For the rest of us, this is the hard part—getting started. We're afraid of looking foolish, afraid no one is interested. We think we can't write well enough. Perhaps we think we shouldn't spend so much time focusing on ourselves. Maybe we're uneasy about remembering or writing about certain times. Let's look at these four familiar and common obstacles.

1. *Someone will think I'm foolish and who would be interested in my life anyway?* If you received *Legacy* as a gift, this particular obstacle can be moved aside, because with this gift comes the heartfelt direct or implied request, "Please write about your life. Please tell me all about you." *But surely nobody's interested in hearing me talk shop!* Even though you may believe that others are bored by talk about special interests or your work, remember that what your interests have been and how you have spent your time are important pieces of the whole.

If you found *Legacy* yourself, you have already taken the first big step. As you sit down to write, trust the feelings that moved you to open this book. Your instinct is sound.

If you continue to harbor fear or to doubt that anyone will really be interested, think of a favorite grandchild or young friend, or a grandchild not yet born. Think about the person a hundred years from now who will pick up this book looking for the connections, the bridge, the assurance that "someone else felt the way I'm feeling . . . maybe I can learn from how they handled it and understand more from how they felt." As you write, picture someone sitting with you, asking the questions. Look at that person, have a conversation, and begin to share your story.

2. *I won't be able to write well enough.* Of course it would be thrilling to produce or read a masterpiece! But, let's agree here and now, that's not the point. What we want, plain and simple, is your story. If doubts arise, continue to remind yourself, out loud, "It's my story, and I'm the only person who can tell it." We'll cover some writing techniques later.

3. *Maybe I shouldn't be spending so much time thinking about myself.* Some people feel that it is unhealthy to dwell on the past, and that it is perhaps vain or arrogant to spend so much time thinking and talking about oneself. It's sometimes hard to see how one's personal history has relevance to the recording of the past that we call history. To these modest souls I would say that the time of reflection on one's life holds an importance equal to that of any other period of life. Your hard-won wisdom and experience will be at hand for family members you will never meet, and the time you spend recording your memories and reflections will be transformed into an unforgettable link to your family and its future generations.

4. *Aren't there some things better left unsaid?* There may be parts of your story you are not ready or willing to tell. Perhaps you fear you might hurt someone by revealing certain information. Only you can decide this. Revealing something hidden, in the still-private process of

writing your story, may show you that the difficulty was smaller than you had imagined, may even bring a resolution you hadn't thought possible.

Perhaps you gave someone a promise of secrecy. Quite likely you'll find it important to continue to honor that trust. But in some instances there might be other factors to consider: you agreed to secrecy because you felt you had no choice; you were too young to understand what was being asked of you; times have changed, and what once we felt it was necessary to hide, we may now be more willing to share. If you feel the revelation of something you've kept secret could be instructive to someone who faces a similar situation, you may choose to talk about this secret from the perspective of what you have learned by looking back, telling the circumstances without identifying specific people.

In telling something you have not revealed before, you may find that your revelation can bring understanding to others confused or troubled by past behaviors or events. With the advantage of the wisdom that comes with the passage of time, it is also possible that in recalling something painful you will see things in a new light, letting go of much of the pain. Miraculously, you may ease into the relief of forgiveness.

So while this writing will be helpful to others it also often helps us to make sense of and peace with our own lives. Be reassured that when you are reviewing the times that were difficult or painful, the choice is always yours to make when you consider the question—"Will sharing this part of my story help more than hinder, and heal more than hurt?"

Now put your obstacles behind you, and let's get started!

The Practice of Writing

Choosing a writing book. I want your finished Legacy to have your imprint from cover to cover. That's why this is not a workbook, but is designed to be used with a blank writing book. Choose a writing book that is easy to use: one that will lie flat and is a comfortable size, at least 5x7, and 7x10 is even better. Notebooks, journals, binders, and various writing books (made with acid-free paper, if possible) are plentiful at office supply, stationery, and book stores. The coated-wire spiral-bound design with its heavy black or colored cardboard cover is a handsome choice at a reasonable price. As time goes on you may want to personalize the cover with your name and a photograph, applied with paste or photo-corners. A large envelope pasted to the inside cover would be handy for photographs, old letters, etc. The most important consideration is to choose a writing book that you like.

Choosing the time and place. Where do you feel most comfortable and sometimes daydream—settled in a favorite chair or sitting at a table? Choose a recalling/writing spot where you feel relaxed and content. If convenient, add soft music that can help you drift back. The more you allow yourself to relax, the more you'll recall. If you think you should write only when the spirit moves you, give that spirit some attention. Greet it with consistency. A set routine will reinforce its sense of importance—first thing in the morning for half an hour, with a cup of tea between ten and eleven every other day, Sunday evenings, or late at night. Set a date with yourself and *Legacy*, whenever and wherever you choose. A date that you'll keep, even if the spirit doesn't *seem* present.

Techniques for Getting Started. The very first session, start at the beginning of *Legacy* by warming up with the first two questions. Then consider the third question: *"What are your earliest memories?"*

For subsequent sessions, many people have found that beginning with the following simple exercise works well for them. With *Legacy* in hand and your writing book in your lap or on the table, choose a section you'd like to work on and select a question. Read the question once again, then close your eyes for a few moments. With your eyes still closed, take a few deep breaths, quietly saying the word "relax" as you slowly breathe out. Now repeat this, substituting "I remember" for "relax." With your eyes still closed, using the name you like to be called, ask yourself the question you have chosen. Let yourself drift back to that time and as you start to see images, hear sounds, smell or feel something familiar, open your eyes and begin to write. Beginning each writing session with this exercise will help you focus and make the shift from your usual thoughts and activities.

As you reflect on the question, try jotting down first thoughts or images, anything that comes to mind as you read the question. For example, one woman noted these fleeting first thoughts at the top of her page when she considered the question "If you were to visit with your grandmother or grandfather, what would that have been like for you?"

> grandmother . . . holidays . . . Sundays: be quiet, no bare feet, sit still, white wavy hair, soft cold perfumed skin, tight smile, straight back, criticisms. . . .

She then picked one thought, Sundays, and began to write, using some of her other images as memory expanded and more details came to mind.

> Every Sunday, my whole family had to visit Grandmother. We children always complained and mother always reminded us the ordeal would last only about fifteen minutes, then we would be free. Sitting on the scratchy wool chairs, we waited to endure Grandmother's questioning. We knew she expected silence until asked to speak. We also knew that if we weren't careful, she'd find a way to slip in a crit-

icism, and mother would defend us as we tried to figure out what to say while our father would look at us and try to remind us with a wink that this was not to be taken too seriously. If we accepted Grandmother's inquisition politely, we would be excused to go out to the kitchen where exuberant Amelia waited for us with cokes and cookies, and then we would be ignored and free to run, roam, and poke around the garden, the attic, or any of the rooms as long as we stayed out of sight while the grown-ups continued to talk. I didn't trust my grandmother and was always relieved but wary if she said something nice. My father would tell me she "just doesn't know any other way to be," which I'd remind myself, but the effect wasn't lasting. I did my best to never get caught alone with her.

This technique of jotting down first thoughts or impressions also works if a subject seems too big or distant. Writing on one small piece of it is often enough to start the memories flowing.

Another approach that works well when you think of a time or an event is to describe what you are experiencing as if you are there, in that time. When the woman who wrote the previous piece tried again from the perspective of a seven-year-old, she found more details. Both versions are in her Legacy. Relaxed, with her eyes closed, she sat quietly for a few minutes and pictured herself younger, and younger, until she had an image of herself as a child in her grandmother's living room. Slowly, she opened her eyes and began writing:

I'm 7 years old, squirming in my chair. This wool seat scratches against my bare legs. It's bad enough we have to visit Grandmother, but it's even worse, when we could be in our fort, to be here, dressed up and wearing shoes. I look at my brother and he rolls his eyes and my sister is trying to ignore us both, because she's the one Grandmother is questioning. About school. The school part I wouldn't mind, but she always asks me if I'm keeping my room neat. She doesn't ask anyone else about their room, but she saw my room once a long time ago when I wasn't home, and I guess my stuff was all around. She called it "a disgrace." I can't say it's neat, because I didn't actually *straighten* it today. If I say it's not neat, she'll say something mean again, and then look at Mommy as if she's the one who has a messy room. I don't know what I should say. When she asks me things that could turn bad, I usually don't answer and look at Mommy and she smiles at me and quickly talks about something I'm doing that's good.

Daddy is sitting quietly, with his knees crossed and his foot slightly rocking. He has a little smile on his face like he's watching something funny. He winks at me, and kind of laughs without making any noise. Grandmother didn't see but I better not look at him again.

Is she almost done? I want to go out to the kitchen where Amelia is waiting with her big hugs and cokes and maybe those little cakes that look like presents. I love those. She's always *very* happy to see us. Mommy told us that Grandmother said, "Sometimes I think the children care more for Amelia than they do me." I asked: "How'd she find out?" Now we have to be careful not to mention Amelia or ask about the cokes. Sure it's true, and I've been worried for awhile that Grandmother will ask me if it is.

"Your mother tells me that you are helping in the school library." "Yes," I answer. I love the library and Miss Page, the librarian. I am her assistant. I smile at Mommy. This is good! "It always is important for one to be familiar with the library. I would think it is very important to keep all those books neat and tidy and on their shelves, now . . . wouldn't you agree?" "Yes," I answer carefully, and look quickly at Mommy. She's already saying something to Grandmother. I wait. I'm not breathing. I see myself standing in the middle of the library with books all over the floor.

Suddenly, Grandmother says what we're waiting for: "I think

Amelia might have something for you children in the kitchen. You may be excused." Now, just the kiss on her cold cheek, and I can leave. Don't rush, walk. My brother says that if your heels hit the ground first you are still walking. Mommy says we also have to be moving quietly and straight up, not bending forward, not shoving. I can hear our heels softly hitting the carpet as we pick up speed. As soon as we round the hall corner, we'll race. Amelia is waiting.

This brief remembrance doesn't give a full picture of her grandmother, but later, she went on to write quite a different picture of her from the perspective of a twenty-one-year-old. The writing kindled a new desire to know more about her grandmother and the life she had led. In writing your Legacy, you have opportunities to comment and reflect on subjects and people in several different ways, so as whole a picture as you know and remember emerges.

Writing on one subject will often bring other memories to mind. Jot a note in the margin and come back to those thoughts later. A man writing about a Thanksgiving remembered his uncle arriving in a new car, the only car in their family. Later, going back to the memory of the car, he saw himself sitting in the back seat—traveling on a special summer trip to a lake, to his aunt's funeral, and to his high school graduation. All these glimpses revealed rich details of his family and his youthful dreams.

Details may seem uninteresting or insignificant to you, but *they are important*. Pay attention to them. Your reader will find them more meaningful than general descriptions. If you write statements such as "I always felt comfortable with my Aunt Louise" or "I didn't like to be alone," take yourself further with those thoughts, tell us *why*. "What did Aunt Louise do, what was it about her that made me like to be around her?" "What was I feeling when I was alone, what did I think would happen?" If you feel uncertain about some of what you are recalling, begin those writings with the phrase, "As best as I can remember . . . " Let your writing reflect the search in your mind: "I just remembered . . ." or "Now another thought occurred to me."

Legacy *Questions*

Legacy questions make it easier. There are a lot of them, each having distinct and sometimes subtle differences. Notice how they draw from you your fullest story. Sometimes you'll cover two or three questions in the same writing piece. You may find yourself hopping between sections, but you'll find their chronological arrangement supports both clarity and recall. If you try the first few questions and are still hesitating, choose any question from any section that sparks a memory. Start there. Once you get rolling, you can always go back to the beginning. You choose which ones you're ready for and how much you want to write. As you write, include a reference to the question. Avoid giving one-word answers. You'll leave everyone in the dark! Remember that your reader wants to know not only what happened but how you felt about it at the time.

Along the way, you'll be nudged and encouraged by quotes from authors with whom you may be familiar, and you'll also meet people I have known or met over the last ten years who have been willing to share excerpts from their own memories and *Legacy* writings. Their stories have always moved me to want to hear more, and to encourage more people to write their personal histories—for all the reasons we've talked about here, and more. Just the other day, when I read back the words of my seventy-four-year-old friend describing her relationship with her husband, she sat quietly for a moment and then said, "I feel as if I have found a new language."

Now You're Writing!

Write in your natural style of speaking. Your own language gives the truest story. Remember, some of the people reading your Legacy will never know you, so your own writing will be the only conversation they ever have with you. Write a little every day, or at least consistently. You'll begin to find your rhythm. Remember, you're giving us your story, not necessarily creating a literary classic! Put your internal critic on hold and keep writing!

Occasionally you may get stuck. When that happens, look deeply into photographs or handle an object connected to the time or person you are trying to describe. Read some old letters, look through a yearbook, or listen to music connected to a certain time. Concentrating on one stage of your life at a time will stir up rich details and feelings. You may well stay with one stage for weeks. Be sure to go back later to some of the questions you skipped. You may be ready to include them. But by no means should you feel that you must answer all the questions in a section; this is *your* story, and *Legacy* questions are intended only as guides to recording what *you* remember as significant in your life experience.

Think about the things in your life and what they meant to you. Houses, toys, cars, books, special gifts received and given, are not merely material objects but repositories of memories often rich with emotional significance.

Now look back with tenderness and courage and write from your heart, and perhaps someone, someday, will find what he or she needs to live life with more understanding, compassion, confidence, and acceptance.

How to Read Legacy

One more point. In *Legacy,* I use "standard terms": parents, mother, father, grandparents, grandchild, children, marriage. Don't take me too literally.

When I say *parents,* please ask yourself, "Who raised me?" Maybe it wasn't your mother . . . or your father. Use the questions to write about those you consider to be your parents. When I say *grandparent,* you may think of an important older person. Perhaps your grandparent was someone else, *grandparent-like* ?

Many people who have not raised their own children have played important and loving roles in the lives of children. Use the sections on "Being a Parent" and "Being a Grandparent" to write about these relationships. The same is true for any standard or conventional term for relationships—adapt them to fit your life.

"Marriage" refers to any enduring couple relationship.

When *Legacy* refers to a specific experience or place, you may have experienced several. Include them all—homes, marriages, schools, jobs, etc.

Remember, *Legacy* is about *your* life! Make *Legacy* work for you.

To my mother, Laura, who wondered what to write,
to my sister, Pam, who knew the worth of Mother's memories,
to my daughter, Laura, who has always asked the questions.

Beginnings and Childhood

As a child, I had to dig to get stories from my parents' childhoods, and the results were scanty. I pestered my mother, "*Where* did you ride your horses?" "Oh, I'd just ride." Then I tried my dad, "Did you wear cowboy boots? Could you twirl a lasso?" Amused chuckle. "Well, *did* you? *Could* you?" "Don't reckon so." Big smile. A man of few words, and 'reckon' not one of them, he was in no rush to dash my fantasies about a life on horseback.

Often I chose the wrong times to ask, but I learned that my mother didn't enjoy revisiting her childhood. Many years later, I found a way of drawing out her early years and as we shared her fun and tender memories she also told the stories that made it clear why she didn't eagerly revisit those years. To my good fortune, she and my dad changed the rules and set out to give their children the kinds of memories they would gladly revisit. My grown children still prod, "Hey, Mom, tell us about the time when the frogs got loose in the car and when Uncle Roddy dyed the dinner blue."

As we move through our lives, we carry with us the stories of our childhood. We may change them, forget or deny them, smile or cry over them, but, like charms or spells, they bring back a sense of who we were and how we came to be the people we've become.

Philosopher Jean-Jacques Rousseau said "nature wants children to be children." As children, we were just *being*, while at the same time we were well into our journey of becoming. A very young friend told me once, "You know one of the best things about being a kid? Even if you're not having fun or you're really mad, you know that some things *will* happen that can make you feel good. Like pretty soon I'll be able to ride a two-wheeler. Right now, I can go frontwards but I can't turn. And next summer when I go swimming, I'll open my eyes under water. Last summer I was scared to, but I'm practicing in the bathtub. There's other stuff, too, but right now I like thinking about the bike and the eyes." Important work, this childhood stage. We all did it— with the same fundamental needs but each with our own particular set of circumstances. What were yours?

Here are the questions and quotes to encourage you to tell how you grew, what you learned. Let us know what it was like to be you, to be *in your childhood*.

I believe that every life, irrespective of its events and setting, holds something of unique value, which it should be possible to communicate, if only one can first see one's experiences honestly and then set them down without too much dressing-up. —Iris Origo, *Images and Shadows*

1   List as many names as you can of the family tree. Tell what you
    know or have heard about any of your ancestors, other than your
    parents and grandparents. Where you can, include any birth-
    places, places lived, or significant dates.

    Write Life Path at the top of a fresh page. Now draw a line from
    the bottom corner of your page to the upper corner opposite.
    Use this as a timeline, pinpointing significant times of your life:
    when you were born, started school, left school, moved, mar-
    ried, began jobs; births, deaths, etc. Be sure to include when you
    begin *Legacy* and when you complete it.

2   When and where were you born? What were you told about
    your birth and infancy, and who told you?

*One memory comes up which is perhaps the earliest in my life and is in-
deed only a rather hazy impression. I am lying in a pram, in the shadow
of a tree. It is a fine, warm summer day, the sky blue, and golden sun-
light darting through the green leaves. The hood of the pram has been
left up. I have just awakened to the glorious beauty of the day, and have
a sense of indescribable well-being. I see the sun glittering throughout
the leaves and blossoms of the bushes. Everything is wholly wonderful,
colorful and splendid.*

                    —C. G. Jung, *Memories, Dreams, Reflections*

3   What are your earliest memories?

To set the scene for your childhood, describe some of the familiar everyday details. When did children generally begin school? What do you remember wearing for play and school? What were the main subjects taught and games played at school? Which toys do you remember playing with or wanting? What kind of transportation did your family have? Which were your favorite foods? What kinds of clothes were the adults in your life wearing? Feel free to talk about things you did not like, too.

4   Where did you live during your childhood and who lived with you?

The house was clapboarded, with a slate mansard roof; it stood high on a bank with an oak tree before it and a verandah ran around it on two sides. The windows looked out on the thickets, over the well in the yard, and toward houses two fields away. This was Oak Street, the first house we lived in, in Ballardvale. At first, everything went surprisingly well in it.   —*Journey around My Room, The Autobiography of Louise Bogan*

5   Picture a childhood home—sketch the plan of the rooms, being sure to mark any special place that comes to mind. How old were you when you lived here? See yourself standing outside the front door. Put your hand on the door and push it open. Begin walking slowly through your home and describe what you are seeing. Recall, in as much detail as you can, your favorite place to be. What did you do when you were home alone?

   —Now go outside and walk around the outside of that home, describing what you see, and any favorite spot you liked to be.

—Tell of a memory from
    when you were four or
    five years old.

6   Where did you play?

Describe one of your favorite
things to play with.

What kinds of "make-believe"
do you remember playing?

What did you find amazing as a
child?

What were your daydreams?

*The dog of your boyhood teaches you a great deal about friendship, and
love, and death: Old Skip was my brother.*
                                    —Willie Morris, *My Dog Skip*

7   Tell about any animals that you loved as a child.

8   What nicknames did you have?

The school opened infinite vistas for this six year old.   7
                                    —Pablo Neruda, *Memoirs*

9   When did you begin school?

Recall your earliest memories of school. What do you remember feeling about your first few years in school?

What do you remember learning? What do you remember liking about school?

What was difficult or frightening?

School came to bore me. It took up far too much time which I would rather have spent drawing battles and playing with fire.
——C. G. Jung, *Memories, Dreams, Reflections*

Who was a favorite teacher? Why?

Which elementary school memories stay with you?

*The friends we made in childhood
were the first people outside of our
family who had a real influence on
us. They were our first contacts with
the world beyond our home, and what
we learned from them we've carried
with us throughout our lives.*

— Betty Conway

10 Who were your childhood
friends and what did you most
like to do together?

Who was your "best friend?"

How did your friendship begin?

What do you think you were
given through this friendship?

How did the friendship fare through the years?

11 What did you do when you came home from school?

Who would be there?

12 Imagine yourself during a typical mealtime. What do you see
going on around you? What would you be eating?

Describe a usual evening in your home.

What was a regular Saturday like? Sunday?

13   What kinds of music did you hear as a child? Write of a memory
     that involves music.

*My mother read with no restraint. As if she'd never heard the phrase
"reading to yourself" she'd laugh, groan, cry, and gasp her way through
her books. We never had to ask her to read to us. She'd suddenly call out,
"bring me* Paddle!" *and one of us would race to take* Paddle to the
Sea *off the shelf. There was always a new stack of library books, but we
all favored the treasured old friends. With a spread of five children, we
got to visit these friends beyond the recommended age as there was always a younger child listening to* The Little House, Caps for Sale,
or Paddle.   —A *Legacy* writer

14   What types of reading material do you remember in your home?
     Which books or stories were your favorites?

     Who read to you? Tell what that was like.

     Where did you like to read to yourself?

15   Were there movies or television shows that made an impression
     on you as a young child?

16   Were you ever in a school or community performance?

17   In your family, what were holiday celebrations like—what holi-
     day traditions did you have? Tell of some holiday memories that
     stand out for you.

     Describe a time when you remember your family having fun to-
     gether.

18 Tell about some gifts you re-
    ceived that you loved.

    What was a special gift that you
    gave?

19 What did "being good" mean in
    your family?

20 What work was expected of you
    as a child?

    What else seemed to be expected
    of you as a child, either stated or
    unstated?

21 What do you remember about your childhood illnesses?
    Measles, mumps, the 'flu? Who took care of you and what did
    they do for you?

    Tell about any visits to the hospital. What do you remember see-
    ing and feeling?

*Some of my earliest memories are of the storms. The hot rains lashing
down and lightning running on the sky—and the storm cellar into
which my mother and I descended so many times when I was very young.
For me that little room in the earth is an unforgettable place.*
                            —N. Scott Momaday, *The Names*

2 2 Picture yourself as a child in a neighborhood or town where you lived. Begin taking a walk past the places you remember. Tell what you see as you walk along. Come to a place that held feeling and meaning for you as a child and tell why you think it did.

—Continue to give us a sense of where you lived, telling us about the weather, the terrain, the size of the community, its culture, and their effect on your childhood.

—What did you like about growing up where you did? What didn't you like? What, with the benefit of hindsight, do you see as advantages and disadvantages?

—How did this place leave an imprint on who you are today?

2 3 Who were your neighbors? How do you remember them being a part of your family's life?

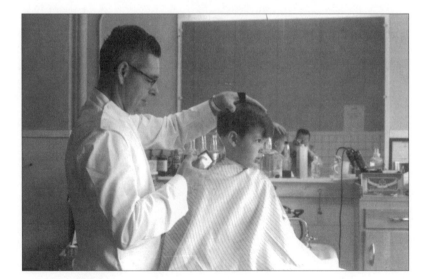

24 In what ways did your parents
    or other adults you knew give
    to their community?

25 What were the historical
    events taking place during
    your childhood and how were
    you aware of them?

26 Tell about a time that was ex-
    citing or adventurous for you.

27 Describe a time when you felt you were in danger.

28 What did you do that you thought you had to lie about?

29 What fanned feelings of envy?

30 Tell of a time when you gained confidence in yourself.

    Write about something you did as a child that gave you a sense
    of competence.

    What did you make that you were proud of?

31 Reminisce about some summertime memories.

    Create a summer evening, filling it with the things you liked to
    do before it was time for bed.

Daddy had some hobbies, and one was kite building. Every spring we would have kite-making day and he would make kites for every kid in the neighborhood. The kites he made for us very little kids were five inch hexagons, out of Christmas tissue and he would tie it just like a regular kite, with a tail and a hummer—the little device glued to one of the strings that would hum when the kite went into the air. Those little kites—we would run along the street, holding them up in the air. Daddy had a workshop out in the backyard. When he died, he had about four or five hundred kite sticks all ready to go for next spring.

—Sterrett Burges, *One Lucky Fella*

Fall, winter, spring—recall some sounds, sights, and sensations from each season. Now choose a memory from each of these seasons to write about.

What are some night sounds you remember?

Few childhoods are entirely without some experience of paradise.
    —Richard N. Coe, *When the Grass Was Taller*

32 Describe the loveliest place you knew.

    What was really pleasing to you as a child?

    What was something you felt you could do forever?

33 What did you do for fun as a child that you still do, or still would like to do?

34 With whom did you share your secrets?

    Where did you go for comfort?

    Looking back, where did you find encouragement in your early years? Whose approval meant the most to you and how did you try to earn it?

    Tell of an instance when someone protected you or spoke up for you.

35 Who were your childhood heroes?

36 What did you believe about yourself as a child?

37 What do you think you had faith in as a child?

    What did you take for granted?

38 Tell of an instance when you felt important.

As she told me the stories, I sometimes sat at her side, leaning against her, or I would crouch on my knees behind her back and lean over her shoulder. As I did this, I would occasionally sniff at her neck, or behind her ears, or at her hair. She smelled sometimes of lemons, sometimes of sage, sometimes of roses, sometimes of bay leaf. At times I would no longer hear what it was she was saying; I just liked to look at her mouth as it opened and closed over words, or as she laughed.

—Jamaica Kincaid, *Annie John*

39   As precisely as you can, tell about a particular experience in which you felt loved.

Who provided your strongest sense of love during this stage of your life?

What would you recall to describe where or with whom you felt safe?

How did you know whom you could count on?

What kinds of affection did you receive that you liked, and from whom?

How were you praised, how were you punished, and how did you respond?

Who or what helped you develop your sense of right and wrong?

40   What were some of your fears?

—How did you hide your fears?

—What response did you usually get if you expressed them?

—Tell about a specific time when you were very frightened.

The wind had been completely knocked out of me. I can still remember my inability to move, the look of the gravel at eye level, and the laughter of the children around me.

James McConkey, *Court of Memory*

41 How did you hide the hurt you felt as a child?

—How did you let it show?

—Tell about a specific time when you felt very hurt.

42 What are some of the times when adults let you down?

She was my mentor, my miracle-worker, and the mother of much that I was and in countless unrecognizable ways probably still am, yet I don't know where she came from or anything about her life apart from the few years of it that she spent with us. Nor do I know what became of her after she left, and there is a sadness in not knowing, in thinking of all the mothers and fathers we have all of us had who, for the little we re-member them, might as well never have existed at all except for the deep and hidden ways in which they exist in us still.

—Frederick Buechner, *The Sacred Journey*

43 Describe any adults other than your parents or grandparents who played an important part in your childhood.

44 Tell about the spiritual life of your family. Did you go to ser-vices? Who in your family went? Picture yourself there and de-scribe what you are seeing, hearing, and feeling.

—What were your spiritual wonderings and beliefs as a child?

45 Tell about the talents in your family.

What were the tales told about the heroes and villains in your family?

46 Reminisce about some family get-togethers—what is the event, what are the adults doing? The children? Describe some scenes that stand out in your memory.

47 How did you spend vacations as a child? Did your family take va-cations together? Tell about a favorite place to visit.

Describe a family trip that you enjoyed. Were there any that were not so happy?

48 What was the first time you can remember being away from your family? Describe the occasion and your feelings at being apart.

What times of separation do you remember as especially stressful? enjoyable?

49 In your circle of family or friends, whom did you dislike and why?

Tell us about your favorites.

50 What subjects were avoided in your family?

—What did you hear about marriage and divorce?

—What did you hear about politics?

— In your family, what did you see or hear about sex?

—What did you hear about money?

51 What were some of the rules your family had?

52 What questions did you have that didn't seem to have answers?

53 What were some of the things you wanted to do as a child but could not?

—Which of them were you forbidden to do?

—Which of them were unavailable or unaffordable?

—What activities that you wanted to pursue were beyond your abilities as a child?

54 Remember a painful or sad time for you. What was going on? How did you respond and what do you think helped you through?

Everyone tells me I can't remember when Sarah died, that I was too little. But they're wrong. I was only three, but I remember. —Leslie

55 Describe your first close encounter with death. What did you see happening, hear people saying, and what was said to you? What do you remember thinking and feeling?

56 What do you know about your grandparents' lives?

Grandmother was essential. She shaped all of us, willy-nilly. She was there the way books were, or spoons. I don't remember ever kissing her or even feeling her hand, but often I held a skein of new yarn for her while she wound the ball, and then leaned my head against her knees as she read good stories from the Bible.
—Elizabeth Coatsworth, *Personal Geography*

What do you personally remember about your grandparents?

I was his wonder because he wanted to finish life as a wonder struck old man. He would call me "his tiny little one," in a voice quavering with tenderness. His cold eyes would dim with tears. Everybody would exclaim "That scamp has driven him crazy." He worshipped me. . . . I don't think he displayed much affection for his other grandchildren. It's true that he hardly ever saw them and that they had no need of him, whereas I depended upon him for everything: what he worshipped in me was his generosity. —Jean-Paul Sartre, *The Words*

57 What do you remember feeling about your grandparents?

—What do you think they felt about you?

If you were to visit with your grandmother or grandfather, what would that have been like for you?

How do you remember your grandparents behaving toward each other?

58 What did you hear about your mother's childhood?

She was a woman who woke early, no matter how late she went to bed the night before. Every morning she would exercise, bending and lifting and touching and stretching, while I sat on the bed watching her with my legs curled up. She ate toast with cottage cheese, standing up, reading the morning paper. But she would always have too little time to finish her coffee. I would watch her taking quick sips as she stood at the door.   —Kim Chernin, *In My Mother's House*

59 During your childhood, what were the things that you're aware of that your mother did in a usual day?

My mother also taught me many other humble crafts—for example, how to drive a nail, how to make paper boats, and how to sharpen a lead pencil.   —H. L. Mencken, *A Choice of Days*

How do you remember her being a mother to you as a child? Describe as specifically as you can a memory of her as your mother.

21

Drift back to your childhood and imagine that you have quietly come upon your mother doing something she enjoys. What is she doing and what does she look like? How do you feel as you watch her?

What seemed most important to her and how could you tell?

60 What did you hear about your father's childhood?

61 During your childhood, what were the things that you're aware of that your father did in a usual day?

How do you remember him being a father to you as a child? Describe as specifically as you can a memory of him as your father.

Yet another image: I am restive, feverish, unable to sleep. My father carries me in his arms, paces up and down, singing his old student songs. To this day I can remember my father's voice, singing over me in the stillness of the night. —C. G. Jung, *Memories, Dreams, Reflections*

I loved him, too; though he was seldom an emotionally expressive man, I knew, he was kind to me. He was my father. But also I was afraid of him. Something always lay between us—something unspoken and (it seemed) unreachable. We were strangers.

—Michael Arlen, *Passage to Ararat*

Drift back to your childhood and imagine that you have quietly come upon your father doing something he enjoys. What is he doing and what does he look like? How do you feel as you watch him?

What seemed most important to him and how could you tell?

62 What do you think the financial situation was for your family during your childhood?

What did you see or hear about your parents' work during this time of their lives?

Other than family or work, what were your parents' main interests?

In what ways did you see and hear your parents behaving toward each other?

From your perspective as a child, what seemed to make them happy?

Sad? Angry?

63 What do you think were the dreams your parents had for their children?

64 What sense about marriage did you get from your mother? Your father?

Reflecting on your parents' lives, tell whether you feel they were generally happy or unhappy with their lives.

What attitude about life did you get from your mother? Your father?

65 What do you remember about the births of your sisters and/or brothers?

He showed me how to hold the scissors for trimming the fingernails of my right hand. He showed me how to handle a jackknife without cutting myself. Hardly a day passes in my life without my performing some act that reminds me of something I learned from Bunny. He was called Bunny because he wiggled his nose like a rabbit.

—E. B. White, *Letters of E. B. White*

66 Remember a time when you were glad you had a brother and/or sister.

—Tell about some of the things you did together.

My brother and I fought over who grabbed the biggest apple, who hid the skate key, and where he put my baby picture. . . .

—Kate Simon, *Bronx Primitive*

Tell about the childhood alliances and rivalries in your family.

—How have these changed through the years?

How do you think you were and are different from each other?

67 Recall a time when you were jealous of someone in your family.

Recall a time when you were angry.

68 What do you think was unique about your family?

69 What are some of the childhood scenes that made indelible impressions on you?

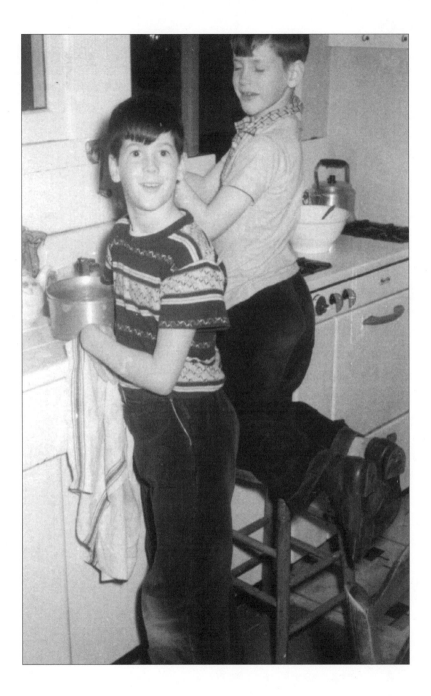

As you look back on your childhood, tell of something you learned that you still value today. How did you learn it?

70 As you are remembering yourself as a child, what do you see yourself doing that holds some of the seeds of who you are today?

71 Do you have something you've saved from your childhood? What do you remember or feel as you touch it?

What would you have liked to have saved?

"Remember that there's nothing higher, stronger, more wholesome and more useful in life than some good memory, especially when it goes back to the days of your own childhood, to the days of your life at home. You are told a lot about your education, but some beautiful sacred memory, preserved since childhood, is perhaps the best education of all."
—Alyosha, in Fyodor Dostoevsky's *The Brothers Karamazov*

72 Which are some of the childhood memories that you most enjoy reliving?

73 Picture yourself as a child. Now imagine this child is standing in front of you this moment. What would you like to say to this child who is now gazing at you?

Adolescence

It's a time of highs and lows: confidence, doubt, trusts, and betrayals. Biology is no longer about bugs; metamorphosis has become personal. Adolescence has begun.

With no one firm step crossing the threshold from child to adult, we dart back and forth with longing glances in both directions. The strong signals our bodies send let us know that we are in new territory, but just where we are in this territory is often confusing. Day and night, sensitive to clues, we test the possibilities. This exploration, internal and external, translates into the emotional hills and valleys of longing, confusion, anger, excitement, pain, love, and fear. It's a time when we feel invulnerable, yet we often, of course, remember times of intense vulnerability.

I remember the mixture: rampant idealizations, comparisons, doubts, convictions, fantasies, earnest desires; the clash of the lingering sweetness of childhood with the enticement of things adult, when I could still joyfully sing old songs with my mom as we drove to the beach for a hot-dog roast, having secretly connived to assure that no one I knew would be there.

Things had changed. In those days, in our school, girls stopped going to the track to run races at lunch time; now we sat on the side and cheered the boys. During vacation, no more swimming in the ocean for hours—we were too busy slathering each other with baby oil mixed with iodine to achieve the perfect tan. And whatever happened to our roller skates and bikes? We walked together to school and to town for cherry cokes and French fries. When we were finally allowed to use the car, after the movies or football games we headed for Oscar's Drive-In for malts—in other words, to see who was there —or we'd just drive around town. Old alliances faded and new ones were made as we found our way in the teenage scene. Drawn to the girls my mother pegged as "more sophisticated," I didn't really fit in, but I liked being included. I don't think we ever discussed anything beyond boys or subjects indirectly related to boys—clothes, makeup, diets, music. As time went on, some dated and some "went steady." For a while, I had an older boyfriend, which made me feel more mature and my parents, I'm sure, more anxious.

One night, there was a party at an older boy's empty house; his parents had moved and he was joining them in a few days, but he hadn't told anyone his parents no longer owned the house. Since we weren't supposed to go to unsupervised "open house" parties, my friend Carol and I went to the movies, but after the show we drove to the party and parked across the street to watch. Sinking low in the seats so no one would see us, we saw her older brother and a boy I dated arrive. There were lots of cars parked along the street, but it looked quiet for an open house and we soon got bored. Just as we decided to leave, police cars raced up, officers rushed the front door, and people began climbing out windows and running in all directions. Hearing commands of

"Stop!" we ducked down, trying to remember from the movies if bullets could pass through car doors. More police arrived and began checking cars with their flashlights; from the floor of the car we heard the commotion of the partygoers being loaded into the police cars. Somehow we escaped being spotted and crawled out of the car and crept to my house. I had no idea what to do, who was in jail, what the crime had been, or if Carol and I would be caught. The next morning at breakfast, my mother innocently said, "Tell me about last night." I started crying. While I was trying to get the story out between gasping sobs, she reached out and touched my face and smiled. Horrified and furious, I screamed, "Why are you laughing at me? Don't you know this is serious?" She answered, "I know, darling; I'm sorry, I couldn't help it. But when you cry your eyelashes get so filled up with tears— your eyes are beautiful." Such relief. I wanted to crawl into her lap. I was safe.

We didn't know it but we were in that quiet time, the last half of the 1950s. The police chief showed a film at a school assembly to warn us about marijuana, the first time most of us had heard of it. Daily television news wasn't part of our lives, although we watched the McCarthy hearings and presidential conventions and elections. I avoided politics at the dinner table; the few times I hadn't, my usually calm father carried on, Mom presented another point of view, Dad escalated his position and ended up swearing and leaving the "damn table." I worried that I'd never have a chance to fall in love, make love, or be an adult because atom and hydrogen bombs were looming somewhere and missiles were pointed right at us. When we learned about the bus boycott in Alabama, cracks began opening in our small world of classes, sweater sets, and doughnut sales. But we knew very few of the painful and serious concerns right in our midst: a friend's parents got divorced, other friends suffered silently with their parents' alcoholism, several girls quietly "moved away" to live with relatives—one of the ways unwed pregnancies were handled. Aside from intensely reporting to each other the meager information we had gleaned, we didn't openly and thoughtfully discuss these matters. Life at the high school went on as usual.

Marking time and feeling out of step, I began to yearn and plan to be somewhere else, and did barely enough to remain included. I wanted the high school years to end. I'm sure many of us felt this way, but we didn't risk exclusion or gossip by revealing our fears and longings.

Recently, as I was thinking about this *Legacy* section on adolescence, I watched thousands of snow geese making their way from one faraway but known place to another, also "known" but still ahead in the remote distance. No question here as to whether this journey would be undertaken. I heard their raucous conversing before I spotted them, wave after wave winging into sight. At first they were faint shadows, then moving clouds of brilliant white, until concentrated focus revealed separate beings, in groups following a leader, a few loners, some pairs. The story of their journey, combined with their utter gracefulness, evoked the same "ohhh's" and "ahhhh's" and "over there's" heard at Fourth of July fireworks displays from us, the admiring witnesses. The flawless grace suddenly broke as the geese approached their options—ponds, marshes, fields. Some were indecisive, some honed in with precision, some hadn't developed their maneuvering skills. They began to slow and lose altitude, wobbling and rocking, legs dangling, big feet spread, skidding, gliding, or plopping onto their landing spot. All the while, gunshots sounded nearby, outside the boundaries of the preserve. The following morning the geese were off again, some leading the way, others taking their cue from the flapping wings around them, pulling themselves up with great and persistent force amid extravagant commotion. The sky filled with their light, a lustrous white sail moving away from us, driven by mysterious and miraculous messages. We stood wonderstruck.

As I thought of the generations passing through adolescence, I wished for some kind of expansive welcoming preserve where there could be safe havens and crash landings and camaraderie and struggling beautiful liftoffs toward wondrous flights. And from a safe and respectful distance, onlookers watching and marveling.

When you respond to the questions in "Adolescence," remember that this section of your Legacy is where young people will turn, looking for fellowship in their suddenly unfamiliar world. So often they do not want, or know how, to talk with their parents about what they're feeling, but they do want a safe place to hear someone's truthful coming-to-terms with living through this time. Someone who has done it.

In setting the scene, you decide the range for the years you consider your adolescence. Again, tell your reader about the world around you by describing the kinds of clothes young people liked to wear; the entertainments—movies, games, sports, music, etc.—popular with your peers; your transportation; the favored food and drink. If you had $5 to spend on whatever you wanted, what would you buy? How about $20? Update your readers on the historical, political, and cultural events taking place during your adolescence, telling how you were affected by them.

1   Where were you living and who was living with you?

Describe what was going on in your family during this time.

2   Where did you go to school? About how many students were in your grade and classes?

Which classes interested you the most?

What interest do you remember having that you wish you had pursued?

What messages were you getting at home and at school about your opportunities?

What did you hear about the education you were receiving and how did you feel about it?

34

In hindsight, what would you add to these years of your education in preparation for the years ahead? What could have been cut?

3   Imagine your teenage self standing in front of your school. Walk through the door—what do you hear, what and whom do you see? What is the first general feeling you have? As you look at the room(s) where you sat, what specific memories come back? What stories can you tell about how you were encouraged or discouraged by your teachers?

4   What were you involved in at school other than classes?

—Describe some of these experiences.

5   Tell about your closest friend. How did you become friends? What did you usually do together? What do you think you gave each other?

—Write about a time when you knew you had a good friend.

—Why has this friendship lasted or diminished through the years?

— How do you feel about this friend today?

Write about your other friendships, how they grew, and what they meant to you.

6   Tell some specific instances of what you did for fun.

7   Write about the music of your teen years.

—Which music was your favorite?

—Where did you hear it?

Which song or piece of music brings back particular memories?

If you sang or played an instrument, tell some of your experiences making music.

8   What were the dances of your day and which did you like?

—Where did people go to dance?

We had two cars in our garage and my girlfriends and I used to sneak my Mom's car out and go to the beach. Once, the two cars were so close we had to bend the side mirror of the other car way back, to get by. When we came back, we couldn't get my Mom's car back in past the other car's side mirror, so I called a boy I knew and he came over and somehow got the car back in place. The next year when Mom started to teach me to drive, she was really impressed that I did so well.

—Sarah Van Dyke

9 When and how did you learn to drive? What rules were you given about cars?

10 What were the rules from adults about dating, sex, alcohol, drugs, and smoking?

—Within your age group, what were the accepted behaviors about dating, sex, alcohol, drugs, and smoking?

—Who or what influenced you most strongly in these areas? What were some of your experiences?

The first time I got kissed I was thirteen. By my girlfriend's brother. I couldn't tell you what it was like. I don't remember. I passed out. Then I ran home. Later I used to have crushes on boys but they never felt the same way. I always felt like the ugly duckling—too tall, skinny, no makeup. I wasn't allowed to date anyway. My mother even put cactus plants underneath my window.   —Juanita Rivera

11 Tell about a crush you had.

Describe a first date with someone, or special time spent with someone you liked.

Tell about a romance you had.

I was 14, in Miss Wolcott's class, and we had to sit alphabetically. While we were waiting for the bell to ring, Susan Bud passed around some invitations to a party and I didn't get one, but the "B's" on both sides of me did. Lance Bird said, "Well, Sarah Blakely is not very popular." I felt terrible. Of course it's laughable today, but thinking of it I momentarily get that same awful feeling.   —Sarah Blakely Brown

12 What did you feel adults or classmates thought about you? Which parts did you agree with and which did you think were not true?

Where did you feel most accepted?

In what ways did you feel competent?

What were the strengths you were learning you had?

What were you learning about yourself at school?

How did you feel you were different from others your age?

The thing to me was to be important, and I tried all kinds of ways. I got a car, I took people for rides, I had a lot of girlfriends and I lied about my age to get a four-to-midnight job in a cannery. I thought with a job I'd be mature. Sometimes the work lasted until 2 a.m., which became a real problem with school. So I just decided to quit school and keep working. The school people zeroed in on me and then spoke to the employer. Since I was going to lose my job anyway, I went back to school. I suppose in some kind of way the desire for importance and maturity is also why I got married at 19. —Keith Lester

13 What was most important to you at this time?

—What was important to you that you kept to yourself?

What did you want to do but could not?

14 Give us a sense of where you were living. How did the weather and location influence how you were living?

Where are the places you used to go
when not at school or home?

15 What did you do that was risky?

Tell about some rebellious actions of
yours. What led up to them and what
were the consequences?

16 What was the most trouble you found
yourself in as a teenager?

—How did you feel about it and what
was the aftermath?

17 What were the family conflicts that you were aware of at that
time? What seemed to be a problem, yet was not discussed?
What effect did this have on you?

How did your family handle conflicts?

18 What work was expected of you? How did you feel about it?
Which chores did you not mind and which did you want to get
out of?

How did you get your spending money?

19 Did you belong to any clubs or organizations?

Were you involved in your community in any way?

When did you begin to feel independent?

When did you feel recognized as an independent person?

20 What are some of the things you did after school?

21 Who were your neighbors? How were they involved with your family?

22 What was the work your parents were doing during your teenage years? What did you hear from them or observe about their work?

—What did you think or feel about what they were doing?

I was boy crazy. Obsessed. I spent much of the day mooning about boy possibilities. And there was an enormous amount of time trying to figure out what was going on between my parents and me. They didn't know a lot of what was going on in my real life and when they asked, I lied. I didn't think it mattered that they knew. I thought I could handle it myself. Besides, they had so much going on in their lives it seemed like I would be imposing to bring them in on my worries. Maybe that's an eternal adolescent thing, I don't know. —Elizabeth Fullerton

23 How did your relationship with your mother and father change during your adolescence?

Recall as specifically as you can some time spent with your mother or father when you were a teenager.

24 Describe any family trips you took.

25 Tell about any pets you had during these years.

26 What did you wish your parents would do for you?

How did you feel you were different from your family?

Write about a time that you felt closer than usual to your family.

What times of support do you remember from your parents or family?

"Why are you spending all that time in front of the mirror? No one will be looking at you!" Beyond a few Oh, Mother!'s I didn't say much but I knew I'd never speak that way to my children. —Joanne Fuller

27 What did you hate to hear?

Tell about your worries and fears.

What pressures did you feel?

When did you feel most at ease?

Would you describe yourself as shy or confident? Give an example to illustrate how you felt.

It's a long time . . . a lifetime since I smelt those particular blooms in that particular summer yet whenever I've seen a currant bush since, wherever I was, and have lowered my face to it, the scent and pink bring the whole thing back. —Sylvia Ashton-Warner, *I Passed This Way*

28 Spring, summer, fall, winter: describe a time you remember from each season.

29 Describe the feel of a summer evening when you were a teenager.

30 What ambitions and dreams did you have about the future?

31 Did you yearn for something to be different in the life you were leading?

—Describe what you were feeling.

32 In whom did you confide?

Who were some of the people you admired at this time?

33 Tell something you did which you thought you could not do.

Recall a time when you felt encouraged by a person or an event.

34 What year did you leave
school?

If you graduated, tell what you
remember about the cere-
mony and any special activities. How do you remember
feeling about this ending and
beginning?

If you left before graduation,
what were the circumstances?
How do you remember feel-
ing about this ending and beginning?

35 Describe an event or time that
was exciting to you during these years.

Describe an experience that still holds feeling for you.

36 Who do you think taught you the most during this time of your
life?

Name something you learned that helped you in the years to follow.

*"Time and again one sees the young exhilarated and restored by the rev-
elation that somebody understands them, feels as they do, has gone
through it and survived, can articulate it and give it form.*
—Peter Marin and Allan Cohen, *Understanding Drug Use*

37 What was the most difficult part of these years and what or who helped you move through it?

38 With the wisdom of age, how would you describe who you were as a teenager? Now tell what you felt at that time about yourself.

39 Recall something you felt was a triumph during your teen age years.

40 What did you value as a teenager?

Which ideals meant the most to you?

41 From your wisdom today, what are you thankful for from that time of your life? As a teenager, what do you think you were thankful for?

Whom would you like to thank, from your adolescent years?

Early Adult Years

"*I was in the service* and had rules and responsibilities but I felt free. It was all I ever really wanted. Having purpose. It meant everything. For the first time I felt 'this is mine.' I was doing something different from my family." Bill Ellis's eyes were shining as he pictured himself in his early twenties. "I remember wearing my uniform home, with my wings, thinking I am different than when I left. I felt like an adult. It was a wonderful feeling, one of the times in my life when I have felt most complete."

As Bill, now in his sixties, looks back at his early adult years, he captures the feeling of what those years were about—going out on your own, finding your way into that grownup world. Even if still at home, in school, or in the military, the twenties are about establishing your independent self.

Karen Sheahan wrote about working and still living at home, when one night she went out with a friend. "He wasn't really a date, we were friends and we had a ball staying up all night and then watching an unbelievably beautiful sunrise. I'd never stayed up all night and it felt very adult. When I got home my father was on the porch, waiting, and

I told him about the night and the sunrise. He said, 'We don't do those things.' I said, 'I do,' and I knew that if I wanted to see sunrises I'd have to break away from my home. I was the first to leave." Karen shakes her head as she remembers that morning and how oblivious she was to her father's concerns—but she still knows it was time to move.

I married in my early twenties. I was in love, and I was also eager to set my own rules, create my own world. For a young woman of my world at that time, marriage was the surest ticket to your own life. Living on your own with a full-time job also bought your entry into that realm of adult privileges and obligations.

Our culture tells us this is the time to take on adult responsibilities and commitments, to produce—a livelihood, a family, a *life*. It is also the time we may be affected more directly by what's going on in the world. War—military service and separation? Economic recession —job shortages? We begin to deal with reality and we have had little experience for what lies ahead. Fortunately our energies are at their peak, as we face new beginnings, try things out, and then try again.

By the time we are in our thirties we're hearing messages about "settling down." For many, this fits, as work and families absorb more and more of our time. These can also be years when we feel powerful and optimistic as some of our dreams become real and the pleasure of this is fresh and strong. That's what Ed remembers. "The war had ended. I'd been lucky. That was already a dream come true, so now I felt that all my other dreams were possible. It's true I felt invincible and I don't know if that was because I came home all in one piece or was it that I was that age and in love and things looked so new and bright."

Others are still exploring, looking for their place in the world. And whether we are aware of it or not, along the way we've made serious choices. By our mid-thirties we sometimes find serious adjustments are in order. Some of us have been settled and come unsettled —our dreams shatter as we grope our way through marriages that falter or fail and jobs that we worry aren't going anywhere or at least not fast enough. As Jack wrote, "When our second child was born I felt panic. I thought, I've got to get serious. I felt I'd been wasting valuable time and I had better start applying myself more to my work. I knew what I wanted and for the first time I also knew I hadn't fully accepted that it was up to me."

We know we're still young and still have time as we face the realization that it is up to us, *we are the adults in our lives*. That realization was absolute for me and totally unexpected. Many of my early adult years were fun, stimulating, and even blissful, very much because of the deep friendship my husband and I had with another couple. It was a rich time together, when we spent weekends filled with lots of laughter, long, good meals, and discussions that lasted until dawn, enthusiastically exploring what we knew we didn't know, and what we thought we knew about life. Our lives changed and became deeply serious when their daughter, the first child of our little tribe, became terminally ill. Their intensely caring parents and aunts and uncles added to the heartbreaking gravity of the situation by being overwhelmingly solicitous and commiserating. To their older relatives, our friends were children, whom they wanted to protect from this devastating pain. To us, our friends were adults, and would somehow bear whatever was necessary for their child's sake.

The new responsibilities of these early adult years deliver a hefty portion of maturing and with that we develop new abilities to help carry us on toward the midpoint of our lives.

These are years in which many people enter into long-term relationships, become parents—life experiences so vital and so multifaceted that it seemed wise to devote separate sections of *Legacy* to each of them. For those Legacy writers whose life experiences include long-term committed relationships or parenthood, it might be easier to separate the interwoven strands of personal history. As you write your Legacy, feel free to turn to the sections on "Marriage" and "Being a Parent" as they seem most appropriate to your own experience and as they best suit your narrative style.

As you write about your experiences of your twenties and thirties, help us see and understand your successes, struggles, and fears, your joys and pains. Be generous, sharing the meaningful parts of your life and giving your reader an insight into how you became the person you are.

During your twenties and thirties you probably covered a lot of ground, physically, emotionally, and socially, moving from one place to another, to different schools, jobs, interests, responsibilities. As you proceed through this section, try to take your reader with you by including in your responses how things changed for you during early adulthood. But first, take some time to set the background scene for your reader. Tell about the popular performers, music, movies, sports, and other entertainments at the time. What fads do you remember? Describe the casual and dressier clothes of the day. What were typical meals at home or restaurants? Give some examples of what $25 could buy. What were the major political, historical, and cultural events of your early adult years? Give the readers of your Legacy a sense of what it was like to enter adulthood at that time.

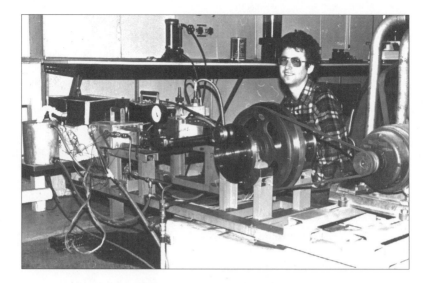

1   What were the significant milestones in your career or personal life in your twenties and thirties?

Tell which you think were thresholds and in what way.

2   If you were in school as you began this phase of your life, why did you choose the school you did?

What was the cost and how was it paid?

Write about the advantages of having gone to this school.

Why did you choose your field of study?

Why would you make or not make the same choices today?

Which classes were a struggle and which were easier?

Tell about a teacher who inspired or encouraged you.

Which were the classes that have added the most value to your life? In what ways?

What were your plans after leaving school?

3   If you were working, tell about your job and why you chose it.

How much were you earning? Give examples of the expenses you had to cover.

Which of your skills were most useful in your work?

What were you learning?

What were your career plans?

If you were to turn back the clock, would you have made the same choices?

Dinner time at our home centered around my father, a warm, witty man who was an avid reader. He would share his opinions on anything from opera to the Civil War. During our college years he began to ask us what we were studying and what we felt. When that happened we knew he was seeing us as contemporaries as much as his children and it felt good.

—Doris Clausius Mosser

4   What was going on in your family at this time?

How was your relationship with your parents changing?

I went across the country to go to college. On the surface of it, it looked like I had left home, but I think it really happened when I went to New

York after college and had some brand new experiences. Things were to-
tally different for me. The process of finding another home was what
those years were all about. Exploring relationships, living in different
places, figuring out what I was at home with. I was aware of feeling a
bit lost, a bit homeless, having left one home and not knowing where
another one was. —Tom Hunter

5 What was it like for you to leave home?

Who helped you prepare to go and in what way?

6 Who were your friends and what did you like to do together?

Who was your closest friend?

—Tell a memory of being together that reminds you of that
   friendship.
—What did you bring to each other's lives?
—How has that friendship endured over the years?

7 Write about your loves—both fantasy and real. When did they
   begin?

My favorite spot, however, was a nightclub nearby. Once or twice during
the week, and on weekends, there was live music there. And I loved it. I
like to hear a singer. Instrumental music I appreciate, but singing I
love. —Mary E. Mebane, *Mary, Wayfarer*

53

8 What were some of the things you liked to do in your free time?

—Which sports or physical activities did you enjoy?
Describe how you were involved in them.

9   What transportation did you have and what did it cost?

10   Tell about any travels you had.

I thought I could do anything. I'd taken my first trip to Europe and my
eyes were opened to a world that I had no idea about—languages, dress,
the distinctive look, sounds, and scents of other countries, my god, I can
still smell Ireland. In those days we were still confined to our own coun-
tries. The world wasn't as accessible. I used to daydream about working
for the government and being an international spy traveling all over the
world. I had a sense of adventure and mystery that has diluted through
the years. I regret that now when you go anywhere, you see too much of

home. Things were more foreign then. And of course, I didn't worry about anything. I thought it's going to continue to be better and better and as long as I adhered to certain rules and regulations I could accomplish anything. How deluded I was.

—Julia Wilkins

11 Recall some of the things that were new to your life during these years.

What were your greatest pleasures during this time?

What was your biggest challenge during this time?

12 Tell of something you did that was adventurous.

13 Tell of something you did that increased your confidence.

14 When did you begin to feel you were an adult?

15 What hopes did you have for your future?

16 What fears or worries did you have?

17 What was most important to you?

18 Describe an eye-opening experience.

19 Tell about someone from these years who was a teacher for you.

20 What were your most difficult times during this period of your life and what helped you through them?

21 What were some realizations you came to?

22 How did your priorities change?

23 Tell how your work was evolving and of the satisfactions and strains associated with it.

24 What causes or organizations were you interested in during this time?

—How were you involved?

25 Which was a road not taken and what are your thoughts about it today?

26 Tell about a time when someone was there for you when you needed them.

27 Within your circle of family and friends, what were the attitudes about marriage?

28 Tell about a disappointment you had and how you dealt with it.

29 What were you thankful for during this period of your life?

Marriage

As a woman who married in the early 1960s, the expectations I brought to my marriage varied appreciably from my parents' time, and vastly from what most people expect today. I did not even consider that it might not last (it did not) and I had scant awareness of how little we really knew each other. Throwing statistics askew, most of my friends and family who married around that time are still married to the same person. What did they know that I didn't? They shake their heads and generously say, "It was luck," because they too knew little of the real person they married. Of course, it was more than luck.

The information we hear most often about marriage today is that it is risky business. The statistics emphasize those that come apart rather than those that stay together. And it is often wondered, which of the marriages that stay together do the partners consider successful? Even with all this, the longing for love and a deep connection with another survives, and some combination of desires inspires couples to make a commitment to each other and begin building what they hope will be an enduring life relationship.

This step in life is optional. And today there are so many options if you do take the step. Within the range of these experiences, is what lies at the heart of successful marriages so different? This is something our stories can help answer.

Couples of the 1990s are marrying in increasing numbers. Informed by statistics and often by personal experience, many are doing so cautiously, thoughtfully, and with passion about the kind of bond they want. These words of Wendell Berry, from his essay in *Standing by Words*, would be a gift to any couple as they vow to be together: "What you alone think it ought to be, it is not going to be. Where you alone think you want it to go, it is not going to go. It is going where the two of you—and marriage, time, life, history, and the world—will take it. You do not know the road; you have committed your life to a way."

With this section, tell those who will read your Legacy what you knew of the way, what you learned of the way, how history influenced you, when you knew it was not you alone, and not your partner alone. Understanding and insights will follow.

I was a senior in high school when I met him coming around the corner to our house. Waiting to go into the service, he was an air raid warden checking on supplies we were advised to have in our homes. He came back that night when we were having dinner. My mother went to the door and I heard him say, "I met one of your daughters today and I'd like to know her better." Mother came back to the table and asked, "Which one of you?" and I thought it must be my older sister, so she went to the door. I heard him say, "No, you're not the one." We dated, but I continued to date others. Before he went off to the war, he wanted to marry, but I felt I didn't know him well enough. Besides, I was young and had things I wanted to do. I wasn't a frivolous girl. We wrote and I dated a lot of fellows and when Bob came back by the end of the war, I was sure. I was attracted to his stability, his strength. I had confidence in him. Well, we were married for fifty years, before he died, and those fifty years were beyond what I had imagined. Was it luck? I think about that. I don't know. It was just a blend that worked. I do believe I was meant to meet Bob that day coming around the corner. —Betty Holt

1   Why were you first attracted to each other?

Why do you think you fell in love?

Tell about your courtship.

When we told her father we were going to marry, he said, "One of you looks happy and the other doesn't." I told him, "This is serious business and it scares me." I never ever wanted to be apart from her and yet I didn't want all the obligation that goes with that, but you can't have one without the other. It's not a fairy tale. It was really her love I couldn't walk away from. She just flat out loved me. —Marshall Saunders

2   What do you remember about the steps that led to marriage?

What doubts or second thoughts did you have?

3   Describe your partner at the time of your marriage.

What characteristic did she or he have at that time that was to play an important part in your marriage?

4   At the time of your marriage, how were you alike?

How were you different?

5   What do you remember about the preparations for your wedding day?

Tell about your wedding ceremony—where it was, who took part in it, and what you remember feeling. What especially stands out in your memory?

What do you remember of the wedding celebration?

6   Tell about your honeymoon. How much time did you have, who made the plans, and where did you go? Write about some memorable events.

7   How did your family feel about your marriage choice?

What do you think you were hoping for from marriage?

8   What surprises did you encounter in marriage?

What is one of the first things you learned about your partner that you hadn't known?

9   As you began your marriage, what were the major challenges of starting your life together?

10 Where did you first live and how did you pay your expenses?

11 What would a typical day have been like in the first year of your marriage?

12 When you married, how did you see your role in the relationship? How has your idea of that role changed through the years?

13 What did you learn early on that was a help to your relationship?

14 What were some adjustments you made?

—Which adjustments do you wish, in hindsight, you had handled differently?

15 What were the most difficult issues to deal with in the early years of your marriage?

Riding down the road in Mike's pick-up truck, on the way to get lumber for the house we were building, I realized that all that I had antici-pated was so unimportant, and other moments held an overwhelming thrill of life, and fullness. At that moment I was a part of belonging. I had never felt so part of something, so connected. —Karen Sheahan

16 Recall some of the best of times from your early years together.

17 How would you describe the early years of your marriage?

18 How did you feel about your in-laws?

—Give some examples to illustrate how you think they felt about you.

Which differences between the two families added to your hap-piness and which were difficult?

19 How were the tasks of providing for the well-being of the home and family divided between the two of you?

—How did your arrangement change through the years?

20 What disagreements did the two of you have in the early years of your marriage?

—How did you disagree?

21 What effect did work have on your marriage?

22 What behaviors or patterns of your parents do you recognize in your own marriage?

—Which were assets? Which were problems?

I learned early on, at Lee's instigation, we had to go out and have dates. We ceased to be parents and went back to being friends and lovers. Spaghetti, the movies, just a little break that took us away from the mad business of parenting and earning a living. It re-energized us. One other thing that was like that: the weekend walks. We went, with the kids, away from our daily life. We left it all behind—the Boy Scouts, Girl Scouts, baseball—and just walked. It was nothing we said, just walking. All fights were forgotten and forgiven and it gave each of us a fresh start. Even if we did it just twice a month, it was enough.

—Barbara Jay

65

23 During a normal week, when would you be together?

How would you get the time to be alone together?

Recall some enjoyable times for the two of you alone.

24 What circumstances would cause either of you to be away from home for extended periods of time?

How did you feel when you were away from each other?

How did the absences affect the marriage?

25 What were the effects of historical events and cultural trends on your marriage?

26 What do you wish you had more of in your marriage?

27 What do you recall as your main struggles during your marriage?

What do you think your partner's main struggles were?

28 What do you think were the main forces keeping your marriage together? In what ways did this change through the years?

29 Which stages of your marriage were the happiest for you?

Tell something your partner did for you that you always appreciated.

Tell something she or he did for you that in retrospect you value greatly?

30 When would you feel closest to your partner?

I can recall every single surprise we ever left for one another. There were all sorts of love tokens, like the spiral of a purple-tinged whelk, a tiny sprig of sea lavender, or a white gull feather.

—Elaine Rothman, "Keepsakes"

31 What are the qualities of your partner that added to your happiness?

What are your qualities that contributed to the happiness?

32 Reminisce about some of the wonderful times together.

33 Describe some common interests and their contribution to your marriage.

In what ways did you support each other to pursue outside interests?

As a couple, in what ways were you involved in the community?

34 Which friends became a part of the fabric of your married life? Tell what they added.

35 What ways did you find to meet your own individual needs rather than the needs of the marriage?

What conscious choices did you make to meet the needs of the relationship?

One may merely know that no one is alone and hope that a singular story, as every true story is singular, will in the magic way of some things apply, connect, resonate, touch a major chord.
                              —Geoffrey Wolff, "Minor Lives"

36 Where did you go for help during the rocky times of your marriage?

What was the greatest crisis of your marriage? How did you get through it?

37 What do you remember of your spouse's behavior before you were married that was a clue to how she or he would be as a partner?

38 The reasons for being together deepen and evolve from the time one marries. What are the reasons you would name at this time?

39 What are some of the things you and your spouse did well together?

40 If you have children, how has your relationship with your partner changed as your children have left home?

41 Describe your most significant times together.

42 What memories of being together do you like to relive?

43 What are you thankful for about your spouse?

How would you describe him or her today?

44 What do you think you brought to the success of your marriage?

What do you understand now that would have helped your marriage?

How did you come to these understandings?

45 What do you think are the keys to a good marriage?

What would you say you have given your partner?

What has your partner given you?

If You Have Divorced

1 What did you think or feel about divorce when you first married?

What experience had you had with divorce?

2　Tell what you feel were the patterns of behavior that contributed to the divorce.

3　What part do you think you played in coming to the point of divorce?

—What would you have done differently?

Tell about making the final decision. What was a particular turning point?

What agreements did you make, legal or otherwise?

4　How did your family react?

What emotional support did you get from family members?

5　If you had children at the time, how were you seeing the effects of the divorce on their lives?

—Describe some instances that stand out in your mind.

How did you try to help your children handle the divorce and the changes it brought? What worked? What did not? How would you do it differently today?

Recall a time when your children tried to help you during this time.

What would you like to say to your children today regarding the divorce and the time that followed?

6   How were your friends a help?

    What reactions from friends were difficult to handle?

7   How did your financial status change after divorce? What was that like?

8   How was your experience different from what you thought it would be?

    What was most difficult for you following the divorce?

    What would you have done differently?

    How was your life better?

9   How did you restructure your life?

10 How have your feelings and attitudes changed toward your ex-spouse since the divorce?

    What kind of relationship did you have after you divorced?

    —How would you have preferred your relationship to have been?

11 Since your divorce, what have you learned that would have made a difference in your marriage relationship?

    What message would you give your ex-spouse today?

12 What was most helpful to your recovery from the divorce?

13   What did you learn about yourself during this time?

14   How have you changed?

If Your Partner Died

Where you used to be, there is a hole in the world, which I find myself constantly walking around in the daytime, and falling into at night.
—Edna St. Vincent Millay

1   How old were you when you became a widow or widower?

As you write this, how long has it been since then?

How long had you been together?

2   Tell us the circumstances of the death.

What do you remember of that immediate time?

What do you remember thinking and feeling?

What specifically helped you get through the first weeks?

There is a sort of invisible blanket between the world and me. I find it hard to take in what anyone says. Or perhaps, hard to want to take it in.
                                        —C. S. Lewis, *A Grief Observed*

3   How did your beliefs affect how you coped?

Which rituals or ceremonies were helpful to you? In what ways?

What type of ceremony do you think would have helped your healing?

4   What resources did you have for bearing your loss?

Which feelings took you by surprise?

What would you have liked others to have done at the time?

What could you have done for yourself that would have made it more bearable?

Those early weeks, the end of daylight was bad. No one sitting there. No one to share silence with or with whom to exchange even idle words. I yearned for Alec's sometimes annoying "come backs."
                    Harriet Robey, *There's a Dance in the Old Dame Yet*

5   What were your fears?

—How have you dealt with them?

—How have they evolved?

6   How did family members handle this loss?

What did a family member do or say that was especially helpful?

What was most difficult for you in dealing with family members?

In what ways were you able to share your grief?

What were your concerns for your family?

7   What did you feel your responsibilities were?

What made you feel angry or resentful?

8   What do you wish you had said "no" to?

9   What offers of help do you wish you had accepted?

I think the best support I received was . . .

What were some unexpected acts or words that you appreciated?

What advice helped you? What advice didn't work for you?

10   Tell about your friends during this time—how they responded, what they did to help.

11   In what ways did friendships change?

12 What advice would you give someone during the first few
    months following a partner's death?

13 What did you do or feel that you thought was crazy at the time?

    Which decisions you had to make seemed overwhelming?

    What did people seem to expect from you that you weren't
    ready for?

> Life must go on,
> though good men die;
> Anne, eat your breakfast;
> Dan take your medicine;
> life must go on;
> I forget just why.
> —Edna St. Vincent Millay, from "Lament"

14 What were some of the things you were able to do when "the
    right time" came?

    What were some of the activities that helped you get going
    again?

15 As life "appeared" to get back to normal, what was the hardest
    part?

    What did you long for?

*My big shock was how alone I felt. No one else was there. When I went
on a trip no one knew if I got home or fell over dead. There was no one*

at the other end of the phone. It was very painful, very sad. If I hadn't gone out and got two little kitties I don't think I would have made it. Now someone was there when I got home—purring at me! They'd demand my attention and I would have to play with them and talk to them. Then they would curl their warm little bodies up beside me. It made such a difference!   —Paula Hardin

16 Give a sense of your loneliness.

What steps have you taken and could you take to feel less lonely?

17 As time went on, what kinds of practical assistance would you have welcomed?

What kinds of emotional support did you miss?

What did you need that you wouldn't let yourself ask for?

Which of your own inner resources do you feel helped you the most?

18 What were the turning points?

19 Tell about the stages of grieving as you experienced them.

Sometimes he's in my dreams. He's just standing there, looking at me. Waiting. He's got on that old blue golf sweater he used to love . . . the one with the hole in the sleeve. Lately he's getting closer. Last night . . . I could smell him.   —Laura Spence

20 What were the dreams that were comforting or illuminating?

In the first few months, when did you feel a sense of her or his presence?

21 What have you kept and why is it meaningful to you?

22 Today, what do you miss most? When do or did you feel the loss the most?

What have you been able to do or would you like to do to live more peacefully with the loss?

What ideas do you have that might help you fill the hole?

Did you ever know, dear, how much you took away with you when you left?   —C. S. Lewis, *A Grief Observed*

23 What were some of the steps you took to restructure your life?

What did you *want* to do but didn't feel you could?

24 How have you redefined yourself?

25 Tell about the new pleasures you have discovered.

I made albums for both our boys. I wanted them to have something to see themselves with their mother, as we were, as our family. But mainly, when the grandchildren are born, I want them to know their Grand-mother.   —Robert Watson

26 Today, in what ways does the family share memories? What would you like to do more of?

27 These days, when are the times you are filled with a sense of your partner?

Which are the times you like to recall?

Which are the reminiscences you'd enjoy with old friends?

What would you like to tell a close, new friend about her or him?

> *The strong root still alive under the snow,*
> *Love will endure—if I can let you go.*
> —May Sarton, *The Autumn Sonnets*

28 What have you discovered about yourself through this journey?

How have you changed?

Being a Parent

"I've always thought we should have some training," Doris mused as she looked back over fifty years of parenthood. As a young mother, I wondered about that too, when, cradling my infant daughter in my arms, I grasped the enormity of this beginning. Why had I had more training to drive a car than to raise a child? Even to me, with my naive confidence, it seemed foolhardy for the world at large blithely to trust young first-time parents with these utterly dependent little beings. After all, the grandparents and aunts and uncles who once could have been counted on for advice and support didn't live just around the corner and we were alone in our neighborhoods with other young parents.

It seems to me that what we immediately learned as parents was how much we didn't know. I was ten when my baby brother was born, and at twelve I launched my baby-sitting business. So, when parenthood loomed, I felt experienced and ready. But becoming a parent was like passing through a veil I hadn't seen before, into a world of instant comprehension. As I looked into my child's face, all the judgments I had made about the behavior of friends who were "over-protecting," "giving in to," or "spoiling" their children evaporated, and were replaced with an overwhelmingly tender sense of understanding. I still wanted to do it differently, but I now felt deeply the pushes and pulls of the emotions that tested other parents and would test me. A retired teacher recalls how in her twenties she was very free with advice to the parents of her students, knowing just what they should do. Laughing, she remembers that after her first child was born, she wanted to go to the homes of all the parents and beg forgiveness.

Parenting is often called a full-time job. Even when it is not coupled with other full-time jobs, parenting takes all the help parents can get. We learn early on as parents how to draw strength and encouragement from other people's stories. We're thankful that this is one area of life in which people seem willing to discuss common experience—especially so if we reveal the fears, worries, and failures along with the joys, hopes, and successes. It helped me to hear of other parents' impatience and sense of isolation during the early years and of their exasperation, worries, and hurt feelings during the teen years. From generation to generation the content changes but the story line continues. My mother worried about polio. I worried about food additives, cultural stereotypes, and creative expression. My worries were swiftly placed in perspective when I thought about hers.

As in every other time of life, the circumstances vary. Being a parent calls for us to be the best we are able to be. When that isn't good enough, when adults fail the child, it may help to consider that they may have done the best they were able to do.

Today's parents turn to professionals more than ever before. Books, television programs, and magazines are filled with the experts' advice. This can be helpful. But it's time to hear from the other experts on parenting—the ones who've done it themselves. Now that you've had some time and distance to reflect on your choices and predicaments, this chapter in your personal history may well provide the following generations with the next best thing to having a wise grandparent on call—moms, dads, aunts, uncles, all of us are helped to find our own wisdom by hearing the truths of others.

1   When were your children born? What age were you when your first child was born?

2   How did your family and friends react to the news?

Compared to how things are done today, I was pretty young when I became a father. Just 24. Up to that point, I'd have to say I was just having fun. Oh, I was working, and I took my marriage seriously, but when I became a father I thought, "everything counts now, everything."

—Len

3   Tell about the feelings and dreams you had awaiting the arrival of each child.

4   What preparations do you remember making for the arrival of each of your children?

5   How did you choose your children's names?

I felt I should know what to do, that it should be easier. It was pretty scary. But then I was surprised how hooked I got; it really was like I was the only person who ever had a baby. I used to sit around all day and look at her. Half the time I forgot to get dressed.   —Connie Fox

6   Tell what you remember of your earliest moments with each child.

7   Describe the day each child arrived. If you adopted children or if you have stepchildren, provide in addition whatever details you know of their birth.

—Where was your child born? At home? At a hospital? How did you get there?

—What was the weather like—any exceptional conditions?

—Who was present at the birth? What were their roles?

—What unexpected events occurred?

—Describe what you know about your child's birth—difficult? premature?

One day, I went around cleaning and arranging all of Megan's little areas: where I bathed her, where I liked to feed her, where she napped. I thought how good and responsible I was to have done that. Then it hit me. I'm the parent. This is it. Up to that point I remember half knowing I was the mother and half thinking I was playing with a doll again.

—Anne Dunbar

8   What were your early surprises about parenthood?

9   How did your family respond to your new child?

10   Who had which responsibilities in caring for your children?

I don't remember my father. And that scared
me about being a father. How could I know
how to be one? But I also thought that by
being a father—the father I wanted—I'd
finally have a father. —Samuel

11 What did you most want to be or do
    as a mother/father?

    What dreams did you have for your
    children?

    —How did you try to bring these
        dreams to life?

12 When did you begin to notice family traits and what were they?

    Which do you think may have been inherited and which acquired?

13 When did you begin to notice your children's individuality and
    in what ways?

14 Give a sense of what your partner was like as a parent.

15 Tell of any other adults who were important in your children's
    lives.

16 What did you most like to do together as a family?

    What did you most often do together as a family, whether or not
    you particularly enjoyed it?

17 Describe a regular weekday with your young child, before five years of age, detailing the time you would have been together. Try to include any specific memories.

Now do the same for a weekend day.

> *My daughter gathers shells*
> *where thirty years before*
> *I'd turned them over, marveling.*
> —Lucien Stryk, "Awakening"

18 Recall one small memory of your young child when you were flooded with a sense of love.

19 What were some of the pressures in your life that stretched your ability to be the kind of parent you wanted to be?

20 How did your relationship with your spouse change when your first child was born?

21 What adjustments did each family member have to make as the family grew?

    For each addition to your family, who found it the hardest to adjust and how did you try to help?

22 What behavior did you expect of your children in early childhood? In their teen years?

    What rules did you have for your children in early childhood? In their teen years?

    How do you feel about some of those rules now?

    Did they have the desired effect?

23 How did you punish or discipline your children?

    How did you praise them?

24 What chores were your children responsible for doing as youngsters? In their teen years?

25 What resources did you tap for learning more about children and parenting?

    —Which advice was the most helpful and where did it come from?

    —Which do you remember rejecting?

26 Recall a summer, fall, winter, and spring memory with your children.

27 How did you spend vacations when your children were young? How did that change through the years?

   —Describe in detail at least one vacation that stands out in your memory.

28 Describe your favorite places to visit as a family when your children were young.

   How did that change as your children got older?

29 Which holidays did your family celebrate, and how? Describe some particularly memorable holiday celebrations.

30 How did you celebrate birthdays?

   —Describe a memorable birthday for each member of your family.

31 Describe family mealtimes when your children were young. Who was there, what were some of your family's favorite foods, and what did you talk about?

   What were meals like as your children got older?

32 Which were your easiest years as a parent?

   Which were the hardest?

   Reminisce about several incidents from each.

33 As a parent, which were the most difficult issues of early childhood? the teen years?

34 How did your financial circumstances affect your parenting and
family life?

35 When your children were growing up, what interests did you
have beyond work and family?

What would you do to find time for yourself? What do you wish
you had done more of just for yourself?

36 What, at that time, did you wish you had more time for? Looking back, what would your answer be today?

37 What were the major differences between your upbringing and your children's?

What did you feel was important to carry on from your childhood with your children?

What did you want to avoid from your childhood?

38 What did you feel was important to teach your children?

What did you learn from your children?

With Kiki's death we were changed. We were different parents. Suddenly we were what we thought we had been. We didn't take our children for granted. We were so grateful for them. We understood we had them to enjoy for an unknown period of time. That was the blessing.

—Saniya Hamady

39 What were the major crises you faced?

40 Which childhood diseases did your children catch? Who nursed them when they were ill?

What were their most serious illnesses, and how were they treated?

41 At what times during their childhood were you and your children apart? What were the circumstances and what was that like for you?

42 Where did you live during your child's early years?

When and where did you move, and what were the circumstances?

What was that like for your children?

43 How do you think historical/cultural events influenced your role as a parent?

44 Were you able to give time to your community? In what ways?

45 What schools did your children attend, from preschool through high school?

Where were the schools located, and how did your children get there?

46 What was your opinion about the education your children were getting at school?

How did it compare to the schooling you received?

47 How were you involved in your child's school experience?

48 What were some of your child's out-of-school activities?
—Music or dance lessons?
—Sports?
—Hobbies?
—Clubs?
—Other organized activities?
—Other individual activities?

49 What did your child feel passionately about?

50 What interests did your child share with you? with your partner?

If you have two or more children, what interests did they share with each other?

—What rivalries and alliances developed?

—Describe, for each of your children, a time when he or she helped a sibling to achieve a goal or overcome an obstacle.

51 Who were your child's friends at different ages? What did they do together, and did you approve?

52 Who were your family friends and what did you do together? How did they add to your life?

53 When your children were growing up, what worried you about each of them, that never happened?

Which fears were sometimes confirmed?

54 Tell of a time when you were most worried or frightened as a parent.

55 How did you deal with changing social mores such as smoking, alcohol, and sexuality?

56 How did you respond to your children's tastes in clothing and music?

57 Which are the endearing or funny episodes you remember?

We'd take walks and play games, like Chutes and Ladders, and I loved to read to him. Usually in the afternoon we'd curl up on the sofa and read a book or two. Mother used to send us wonderful books and I found myself liking the ones she used to read. Then when he got older, we'd still read, but he'd read to me. —Katherine Barngrover

58 Describe in detail what you most liked to do with your baby.

—your toddler

—your young child

—your teenage child

What do you most like to do with your children now?

What *would* you most like to do with your children now?

59 From the wisdom you possess today, tell of something you'd do differently raising each child.

60 As specifically as you can, describe a time that you spent alone with each child.

61 What did you do to reinforce your child's sense of self-worth?

If you had more than one child, what did you do to give each child a sense of being treated equally?

If you had more than one child, what did you do to give each child a sense of having their fair share of you?

It was just this morning,—I'm stopped at a stop light; I glance in my rear view mirror. The sun is shining on the faces of the passengers in the car behind. A mother and her young son . . . is he seven? eight? They are looking at each other and laughing. I find I'm smiling as I watch them. Still with wide smiles, they say a few words, looking at each other. At the next light, I look back again. They are looking straight ahead now but the smiles are still there and the warmth. I look back, so far back. My child, my dear child, did we have such times together?
—a Legacy writer

62 Tell of something you'd like to do again with each of your children.

Tell of something you wish you'd done more often.

I don't remember teens being so difficult, but I'm sure they were. I remember once I was sitting and talking with one of my daughters. It didn't seem like that much of a conversation. Suddenly she jumped up and said, "You never have understood me!" and went rushing to her room. I remember how startled I was. —Doris

63 How did your experiences as an adolescent influence how you responded to your teenage child?

64 How do you feel your work affected your life with your children?

65 How did decisions that you made regarding your own life affect your children? decisions their other parent made?

—Living arrangements?

—Career plans?

—Personal habits?

66 How do you feel your relationship with your partner (or ex-partner, or new partner) affected your children?

67 At what points did you feel your children were launched into the world and how did you feel at those times?

68 What have been the major concerns you've had regarding your adult children?

Which of your adult children's difficult times have also been hard for you?

—As specifically as you can recall, what have you tried to do during these times?

69 What gives you special pleasure in your relationship with your adult children?

70 Of the choices that you made, which have you wanted to protect your children from making?

—How did you subtly or directly try to accomplish this?

71 Which are some times from their childhood that you enjoy remembering?

What have been your greatest joys as a parent?

72 What do you think were the advantages and disadvantages of your children's childhood?

How do you think their childhood was influenced by the time and place?

73 What insights did you gain from parenthood about your own parents?

My father died so I was raised by my mother and grandmother. I had no clear picture of what being a father was about. I wanted to get a job, get married and have kids. I saw myself as being part of this loving group. I never saw myself as the patriarch. I just wanted to be part of a family. So it happened. Later, I remember one particular point: I used to swat, not spank, but kind of lash out, and I remember so clearly I was walking down the hall, angry about something, and Christine ducked. It's a vivid memory. I knew I didn't want that; I didn't want her to fear me. Then I announced at the dinner table that I would no longer lash out. I kept my vow and it's made a difference, of course. —Walt Creber

74 As parents, we all have some regrets. Which are the scenes that come back to you that you still regret and how would you replay them today?

75 What would you like your children to know about you?

76 Tell of something you admire about each of your children.

77 As you look back on your years of parenting, which are some times that give you a sense of contentment?

78 What were you able to give your children that today brings you a sense of accomplishment or satisfaction?

79 What did you want to give your children that you feel you did not?

80 If you have saved something that was part of your child's life, place it before you and hold it or touch it. What are the thoughts and feelings that come to you?

81 What message would you like to give to each of your children?

82 What do you hope each of your children will always know?

Middle Adult Years

"At last everything was taking shape—my marriage, my daughters, my work," Tom remembered.

> We could afford to have some extras. I remember thinking this is the way it is supposed to be. We'd worked really hard, on all of it, and I know I was lucky, for instance drugs weren't around when my daughters were growing up. I was able to help my mom and dad out, too; I loved that. But you know, I kind of held my breath because I was afraid something might happen. It didn't. But, I remember sitting on the back steps a few times in the middle of the night, going over in my mind if I was missing something that I should be paying attention to. I still feel I was lucky and I was blessed.

As Tom found, it is during these middle adult years that we see the results of the time and energy we've given to our family, work, community, self. The middle adult years, the forties and fifties, while they can be years of stability and widening circles of responsibility, can also be times of assessment, evaluation, and "paying attention."

Sometimes the result of that assessment comes as a jolt, as Michael remembered. "I didn't see that I had much choice. My marriage was coming apart. It was now or never if I was going to do anything about it. Somehow I chose now. I decided to take responsibility." As Michael recalled those earth-shaking realizations of his mid-forties, his eyes teared. He could still easily recall his shock and the following fear as he set out to make sense of his life.

"Mid-life crisis" has become a familiar phrase. In reality, the phenomenon may be less a crisis than a slow awakening, but either way, these years usually involve soul searching. What am I doing? Is this all there is? Is this what I was meant to be? A heightened sense of mortality urges us to wonder about the possibilities. Petey, now sixty, looking back, writes, "I always thought I'd be a real barn burner. When I hit fifty, I realized I hadn't done those things. So far, I'd had a good life and had done interesting things, but I began to wonder if I had to give up on my barn burner image."

This questioning may precipitate radical shifts in thinking and living, or minor changes and quiet risks. Mabré and Anne had differing experiences. First Mabré:

I loved teaching. Loved the kids. I'd teach whatever they needed in the village where we lived. One year I had 45 sixth graders in a basement of a church, with another 45 kids on the other side of a thin temporary partition. We had one toilet and no playground. I remember George in particular, he wasn't a bad kid, just *very* active. And with so many other kids in such a small space, well, the whole situation was unbearable. After that year, I said there *must* be something more in life. I knew a woman who had a career as a librarian and I thought why couldn't I do that. Loved books, always had. So I borrowed the tuition money and drove to the university three days a week. Took every class I could toward my library science degree. I became a librarian. I was 45. I felt I had found the job for which I was born. I have loved it.

Then Anne:

> It was a single compelling event. I heard a human rights speech that brought up very strong feelings. I didn't question long, I got involved. It didn't feel like a new thing but a re-acquaintance with a part of myself. As time went on, I had to give a short speech and moderate an event. I was anxious about it, but I felt I did it well. The next day, someone said I had been really powerful. I liked that. I don't think I had been called that before. It was a reawakening. It engaged both my passion and my intellect.

Anne Dunbar remembers that time and has carried that sense of herself into her sixties.

Anne's and Mabré's brief stories begin to give a sense of what this time was for them—of how their experiences defined them, and to what extent they were able to discover another part of themselves. It is through the details of their accounts that we can picture these events in their lives. We can see Anne giving her speech, Mabré in that church basement with George and all the other kids, just as we can see Tom sitting in the dark on his back steps paying attention to his life. In this section, "Middle Adult Years," pay attention to *your* details, *your* specifics, as you answer the *Legacy* questions. Leave your reader with a deeper sense of who you are.

The past is never dead. It's not even past.

—William Faulkner, *Requiem for a Nun*

*Set the scene again, as you think back to your middle adult years.
Where are you living? What are the accepted roles for men and women
at this time? What political, historical, and cultural happenings were
taking place and how do you think they were affecting your life? List
a few examples of popular music, books, entertainment, fashion, cars,
and food. Spending $25 on yourself, what could you get? Give some
examples of the cost of living.*

1   Give us a sense of what it was like to live where you did by
    telling about the town (country? city?), the weather, the culture.

    Next, sketch the floor plan of a home you lived in during this
    time.

2   Describe your family as you entered your middle adult years.
    Were you married? If you had children, what were their ages?
    Were your parents living?

    Where were family members living? How often did you see
    those who did not live with you?

    How did these circumstances change in the next two decades?
    Describe the major milestones of family life during your forties
    and fifties.

3   Tell about the work you were doing and how you felt about it.

    How long had you been doing this work?

    How did you get the job, and what were you earning?

    About what other livelihoods did you sometimes fantasize?

Concerning your work, what were you planning and hoping for the future?

4   Pick a time during your forties and give a sense of how you spent an ordinary weekday.

   Choose a time during your fifties. How would an ordinary day be different from the one you have described?

5   Who were the significant people in your life?

6   Whom were you closest to?

7   Who were your friends? How did the friendships develop and what did you do when you got together?

Write about a time with your dearest friend that would give us a sense of why this friendship thrived.

—When was a time you were able to help each other?

—What did you do to sustain the friendship?

—Write of a pleasurable memory of being together. Where is this person today?

8   Who were your neighbors, and how did your lives touch?

9   How did you like to spend Saturday? Sunday?

10 What kinds of physical activity did you participate in?

11 How did you like to spend time you may have had alone?

What did you wish you had more time for?

12 Which were some memorable vacations?

Tell about some other travels you had.

13 What are your memories of the significant happenings in your life at this time?

14 What new interests did you have?

15 What activities did you share with your family—children? partner? parents?

What changes occurred over the years?

16 How were you involved in your community?

17 What were the things you thought you'd do when "you had enough time?"

18 What had you saved for that you were finally able to afford?

19 Tell about some of your greatest pleasures.

What did you most value during this stage of your life?

20 In what ways were you continuing to increase your knowledge and skills?

21 What did you feel your priorities had to be at this time?

—Why do you think you made these choices?

22 What difficulties did you have to deal with at this time?

23 What were your worries and fears?

24 What do you recall as personal successes during these years?

What is something you did that you thought you could not do?

25 What would you choose to do differently with the benefit of hindsight?

If I am to be loved or hated, at least I should like the hatred or sympathy to be for the real man. Why don't I try to depict him as I think I have known him. ——André Maurois, *I Remember, I Remember*

26 Where did you invest most of your energies?

27 What was your greatest challenge during this time?

28 Tell about a turning point for you in these middle years, explaining why it held significance.

29 Recall something you took a chance on that you now know was the right thing for you to do.

30 What did you do when pressure and stress built up? What helped the most?

31 What do you think you were learning about yourself during these years?

Give a sense of what you had to be thankful for.

32 Which were the best of times during this period of your life?

Being a Grandparent

When my first child was a toddler, I saw a soup commercial of a mit-
tened little boy tramping out of the snow into a warm kitchen. Sitting
on the oilcloth-covered table were two bowls of steaming soup, but
the big scene was the cozy greeting the child got from the gray-haired
man in the plaid flannel shirt. I admit that this scene became my
grandparent fantasy for my kids. I wanted them to be able to walk
down the street to a house where a grandparent lived. A grandparent
who knew about just-in-time hot food, a toasty kitchen, and I'm-glad-
you-got-here greetings. It didn't work out that way. Not because their
grandparents wouldn't have created just such a scene, but because we
lived on opposite sides of the country, two thousand miles apart. The
weekly phone calls, letters, and yearly visits were so nurturing that
my "just down the street" fantasy was only reinforced. My children
lost their grandparents too young, and I wonder how much they really
remember of the early morning invitations into the big bed, lying together reading while everyone else slept, or of emptying the cup-
boards of pots and pans to see how much rain they could catch. Those
were vacation days, just a week here and there in a year.

Adults I know who spent significant time with their grandparents talk about the experience a lot. It clearly is important to them. Today, however, many future grandparents are waiting longer for that significant time to begin, as their children marry later and postpone having children. Some grandparents, too, feel they finally have the free time to travel and not be tied down. Fit and adventurous, it's not a time they want to give up to baby-sitting. For others, it's more complicated than usual. A friend of mine whose grandchild has eight grandparents must work at finding room in her grandchild's life.

I've heard a lot of good-natured comments like my mother's: "My job now is to enjoy them; I'll leave the rest to you." At the same time, there's an increasing number of grandparents having complete responsibility for raising their grandchildren. Tony Martinez says he is "mom, dad, and grandpa" to the grandson he is raising. At sixty-one, he insists it keeps him in good condition making every baseball practice and game, grocery shopping, taking his grandson to school in the morning and rushing back after work to pick him up.

The need for grandparenting seems to be all around us, with both parents often working long hours and families stretched long distances. Many young people go through life without ever having a relationship, nor even a meal or conversation, with an older person. I met a woman at our local retirement center who, when she moved to California, had all sorts of plans for her newly gained free time. But as she visited with her busy commuting daughter and son-in-law, she realized that what was missing in that family's life was home cooking. She had never had the time to enjoy cooking, but she decided that it would be her gift to her children and grandchildren, and so, for about a year, she prepared their dinners. Sometimes a week's worth would go into the freezer, but they could always count on a good dinner. She got to know her grandchildren as they'd wander into the kitchen after school and nibble or help her chop. She's not doing it anymore, but cooking is her hobby now. She loves to read cookbooks, and once every two weeks she invites family members to her studio at the retirement center for a dinner she has had fun planning and cooking.

Some people look forward to grandparenting as a second chance to be the parent they never were. Seeing my father with his grandchildren was an eye-opener for me. As a father, I knew him to be caring and benevolent but reserved and somewhat remote—he drove the car but he didn't sing the songs. As a grandfather, Popsie, he liked to have his grandchildren right beside him. In the evenings, we got used to seeing him sitting outside having long quiet conversations with a grandchild. Sometimes the child in his lap was too young for any response beyond stares and fingers reaching up to trace the lines in his face; other times you'd hear their voices, grandfather and grandchild, back and forth.

I've wondered if the person who came up with that soup commercial was pulling from a real memory, or, like me, had a grandparent fantasy. I know I want to be free to roam but my desire to be "just down the street" is stronger. As usual, there are many styles, experiences, and unique situations in grandparenting. Please include yours in your personal history. Someday, a grandchild will surely read it.

1   What are your grandchildren's names, ages, and where do they live?

2   Where were you, what did you do, and how did you feel when you learned you were a grandparent?

3   How did you envision yourself as a grandparent?

I love baseball and he loves baseball. I've been teaching him since he was three and it's made it better for both of us. He's a good little ball player. We've got a park nearby where we go in the evening and hit fly balls. Every time we do something, I'm always trying to let him know it's OK, he's just a little boy, not to worry. I make sure I'm there for him. It helps me out in lots of ways. I like to be with him, that's what makes me happy.
—Tony Martinez

4   How are you involved in your grandchildren's lives?

—How would you like to be involved?

5   What is satisfying about being a grandparent?

Describe some specific things you like to do as a grandparent.

6   How did your relationship with your child change when you became a grandparent?

7   How are your attitudes and feelings different as a grandparent than as a parent?

What are you doing with your grandchild that you wish you had done with your child? That you wish your parents had done with you?

What are your challenges as a grandparent?

8   What have you learned as a grandparent?

I expected that I would be a greater part of my grandchildren's lives. I have not been because of distance and I feel a tremendous loss. And now that they're entering their teens they're more like strangers and I feel I don't know how to communicate with them, so I feel real sadness about that. —Lois Riboli

What has surprised you about being a grandparent?

9   What have you learned about your children from seeing them as parents?

If asked, what parenting advice would you love to give?

10   How would you describe your children's relationships with their grandparents?

   —How could those relationships have been better?

11   How did you feel when you were with your grandparents?

12   How would you describe yourself as a grandparent?

What do I want? I want to be there for them, and with them.   115
                                                    —Titia Ellis

13 Tell what kind of relationship you would like with your grandchildren.

What would improve your relationships with your grandchildren?

14 Tell of something you'd love to do with your grandchildren.

15 Have you saved anything from the past that your grandchildren now enjoy?

The big thing about grandparenting is that it does offer all the rewards and benefits you hear about for years. It's true, it's true. I've decided that it is my task, as a grandmother, to make memories. My grandparents were far away in Scotland, and then dead; I never saw them. I'm going to provide a link for these children to my generation. In whatever way I can. I want them to know consciously or unconsciously that there is a link. I consider this to be important. —Patricia Cummins Cooke

16 What would you most like to do for your grandchildren?

17 Tell something encouraging about each grandchild.

18 How would you like your grandchildren to remember you?

Later Adult Years

As I go out my gate to pick up the morning paper, I usually see my eighty-five-year-old neighbor, Bill Pemberton, doing the same, in his red plaid bathrobe and well-worn cowboy boots. He answers my "What's up?" with a few quick comments on the news and his upcoming plans, which could be flying off to a Far East conference, wilderness fishing, a family visit, or simply going to the office with plans to quit early so he can swing by the convalescent hospital to croon big band tunes. His wife, Oma, at eighty-three, isn't far behind as she'll head down the hill to volunteer at the local hospital or fill her basket at the farmers' market. I go back into my house and call out, "I want us to be Bill and Oma Pemberton when we're their age!"

The past ten years, as I've worked with the *Legacy* questions, I've talked and listened to many people in retirement centers, in church meeting rooms and living rooms, and across kitchen tables. When we've focused on the later adult years, it's been very clear that those in their sixties, seventies, eighties, and nineties are today's pioneers. "Life today is so radically different than before when there was no Social Security, not as good medical care, and people didn't live as long,"

Mabré Krueger explains as she compares her life at eighty-two to her parents' and grandparents'. Of course health and finances have major impacts on how the later years are lived, but diversity and trailblazing abound. Mabré adds, "At eighty-two, I'm getting so I have to conserve energy. I have to do things that aren't too strenuous, but if I'm careful and sit down every now and then I can do most anything. My big joy in life is reading. I also love the Elder Hostels. I've been to about fifty of them. I went to one in Wyoming and now I'm so excited about the Lewis and Clark story!" From our elders we're learning new possibilities about what lies ahead.

Doris, in her seventies, still sails on the freighter trips she used to take when her husband was alive. "Recently I went all over Southeast Asia. Now I want to go to Russia and China. At this stage of my life I can do what I want, except my daughters sometimes laugh and say I'm crazy! There's no one to tell me what to do and what not to do. The only problem is . . . very few freighters are taking passengers these days." This was not the kind of problem I expected to hear from someone in her mid-seventies.

Even though I'm still surprised when I hear about the years beyond, I've finally adjusted my expectations about what I'll be doing in my sixties. I see them all around, 60+-year-olds kayaking, hiking, biking, skiing and doing a lot more of what they did, or dreamed of doing, in their forties and fifties.

But there are different ways to be active as possibilities become limited. My mother was not physically well during her last years and died at sixty-nine, but in those years she continued giving to her community and finding joy in life. She expanded her church's Thanksgiving meal into a town-wide event for everyone who had no place to go. She tucked jelly beans and little surprises in the mailbox of a busy mother for her three young children. Whooping and hollering, she shot down a rapids-laced river on an inner tube. And in the last year, in bed or in her wheelchair, her range extended to anyone who came by. Listening and with a caring and time's-running-out honesty, she helped tie up loose threads so lives could be lived with more joy.

We have much to learn from our elders as we watch them inhabit new territories. And our charts and maps are few, as this region of life is experiencing the greatest transformation of any in the life cycle. In thinking about his later years, John wrote, "There are some things you only learn with age. For me it was learning to be truthful with myself. I realized I didn't have time left that I was willing to waste. But you have to discover that one for yourself, because it's different for everyone."

So what are you discovering? Use the *Legacy* questions to share your unique experiences, thoughts, and feelings as you add to the knowledge of life in the later years.

The older you get the more they'll want your stories.
　　　　　　　　　　　—Ellen Kort, "Advice to Beginners"

What is the date as you begin this section?

1　Sketch a plan of where you live.

　　What do you like about where you live now?

　　What would make it ideal?

2　How do you spend a usual weekday? weekend?

3　Describe who you are today.

—How would you say you are different today from the way you
were ten years ago? thirty years ago?

—What significant changes have there been in your life over the
past ten years?

4 How is your life different today from how you thought it would
be?

—What are some of the best parts of being the age you are
today?

—What are some of the challenges of the age you are today?

—What has surprised you about this phase of your life?

5 What is the source of your income?

If you are working, tell about your job.

—Tell what you like about it, what you feel you contribute.

—When, if ever, do you plan to leave it?

If you have "retired," tell about the transition from full-time or part-time job to full-time life.

—What was the hardest part of the adjustment?

—What are some unexpected benefits?

—What do you enjoy most about not going to your last job?

—What do you now do that you had put off while you were working?

6   How would you describe your health?

—What do you do to maintain your health?

7   Who are the family members you are in touch with?

—How do you spend time together?

—Who of your family would you like to spend more time with and what would you like to do?

8   Who are the people providing the most satisfying companionship to you now? What makes it work?

9   Which are the friendships you savor?

Discounting distance and cost, if you could spend more time with someone who is part of your life today, who would that be, and how would you like to spend the time together?

10 How have your adult friendships taken hold?

11 What do you really enjoy doing?

What do you enjoy more today than you used to?

What could you not live without?

What would you do in an ideal day where you now live? What would you do in an ideal day if there were no limitations?

12 Whom would you like to see again, and what would you want to do together?

During much of my life I was anxious to be what someone else wanted me to be. Now I have given up that struggle. I am what I am.
—Elizabeth Coatsworth, *Personal Geography*

13 What do you now allow yourself that you did not in the past?

What do you ask of yourself that you would like to let go of?

14 What are some adjustments you've made to make this time of your life happier?

Thus it is that I have now undertaken, in my eighty-third year, to tell my personal myth. I can only make direct statements, only "tell stories."

Whether or not the stories are "true" is not the problem. The only question is whether what I tell is my *fable,* my *truth.*
                    —C. G. Jung, *Memories, Dreams, Reflections*

15 Draw a line representing your life so far, putting your birth date at one end, and today's date at the other. As you look at this lifeline, place marks along the line indicating significant spiritual points of your life. Tell why they hold significance.

16 At this time, how would you describe your spiritual life?

    What do you need to do to feel you are on your spiritual path?

17 What changes in priorities have you made for this time of your life?

    What matters most to you now and how do you make it part of your daily life?

18 What have been your dominant concerns during this stage of life and how have you handled them?

19 Tell about a recurring or lingering night dream.

    What goes through your mind during wakeful nights?

20 To whom do you turn for comfort and guidance?

    —Tell of an instance of this support.

21 What do you need to feel content?

I have more daydreams than for many years I had time for, but usually now they are in the form of memories, not longings.
> —Elizabeth Coatsworth, *Personal Geography*

2 2   Lately, what do you find yourself daydreaming about?

Which are the sounds, sights, or scents that set off memories for you?

What comes to mind when you say, "I can still hear the sound of . . ."?

—It may help to sit back, close your eyes, deeply and slowly breathe in and out three times, then slowly say the phrase "I can still hear the sound of . . . ."

2 3   Where have you had your strongest sense of home?

Tell about a place that's meaningful to you that no longer exists.

I think now, in looking back on these summer trips——made in the car and on the train——that another element in them must have been influencing my mind. The trips were wholes unto themselves. They were stories. They changed something in my life; each trip made its particular revelation, though I could not have found words for it. But with the passage of time, I could look back on them and see them bringing me news, discoveries, premonitions, promises——I still can; they still do.
> —Eudora Welty, *One Writer's Beginnings*

24 Tell of a memorable trip you've taken.

Describe an experience of being in a place of scenic beauty or natural wonder.

What is a trip you'd like to take?

25 Who has provided your strongest sense of love during this period of your life?

26 What attitudes and beliefs have you changed regarding men, women, parenting?

What do you think are the misconceptions that younger people have about people your age?

What changes would you like to see that would benefit your age group?

27 What are the social and political issues that have most concerned you throughout your life?

What current issues interest you the most? Tell why they are either distressing or pleasing.

Tell us what the significant historical and political events of these times are. In what ways do you think your life is affected by them?

What changes would you like to see that would benefit the younger generations?

28 In what ways do you think people of your generation can make contributions of time and skills? Which ones interest you?

Tell of any ways you have found to give to your community during these years.

Whom do you admire for the contribution they are making now?

29 Was there a time when the "kindness of strangers" (or someone only slightly known to you) made a difference in your life?

30 What do you feel you are still learning?

Who are your teachers today?

What have you learned in the last five years that surprises you?

31 Write about any turning points in this stage of your life.

The story and study of the past, both recent and distant, will not reveal the future, but it flashes beacon lights along the way and it is a useful nostrum against despair. —Barbara Tuchman, *Practicing History*

32 How would you redo some of the moments you regret?

33 What would you like to stop doing and why?

What would you like to start doing?

How do you think your life would be different with these changes?

34 What makes you mad?

35 What are your challenges today?

What potentials have you lately discovered?

What are your strengths?

What are you exploring?

What is an adventure for you?

36 Recently what is something new you've tried or thought about trying?

What are some things you've longed to do and never done?

37 What would you like to be doing with your grandchildren or someone of a younger generation?

38 What do you worry about?

—What do you think you would do if you didn't hold these worries?

39 What changes would you make in your life today to make it more satisfying?

What do you resist?

40 What has always seemed to come easily to you?

Which are the parts of your youthful self that you have re-claimed for your life today?

41 Reflecting on the interests you've had in your life, trace them back to where you think the sparks were struck.

What ignites your creative spirit today?

Describe some specific moments of beauty in your life today.

Today, which are the moments of awe and wonderment?

42 Which are the values you've had that have endured or strengthened as you've grown older?

43 What is something you could do for someone else that would give you the most satisfaction?

44 Write about the things that bring you personal satisfaction today.

Memory is valuable for one thing, astonishing: it brings dreams back.
—Antonio Machado

45 How have you changed your earlier dreams?

What dreams did you feel you had to leave behind?

Which of your dreams remains intact?

46 What feels unfinished that you would like to resolve?

*In the past few years, I have made a thrilling discovery . . . that until
one is over sixty, one can never really learn the secret of living. One can
then begin to live, not simply with the intense part of oneself, but with
one's entire being.* —Ellen Glasgow, *The Woman Within*

47 Which are some gains you've experienced that you really
wanted?

Which are some ongoing hopes?

48 What strengths and trusts would you need to live the wisdom
you have gained?

In what ways do you feel you are already living from your
wisdom?

49 Okay, you have five wishes. They will come true. What are they?

*All these things and a thousand more are embodied in me, the good and
the bad, the wide rings of growth and the narrow. One's past isn't something we leave behind, but something we incorporate.*
—Elizabeth Coatsworth, *Personal Geography*

50 As you look back on the life you have lived so far, what are you
most respectful of?

51 Tell a story from your life that you've never told before.

52 What do you have faith in?

53 What are you grateful for during this time of your life? Give a sense of why this is important to you now.

54 How do you feel about your life right now?

55 What are you looking forward to?

Reflections

Recently, I visited with some people in their late eighties and nineties, who are no longer very active. As they talked about things they used to do on a free summer's day seventy to eighty years ago, their voices grew stronger and their bodies more animated. The river, the picnics, the horses, the singing, the trains full of soldiers—the tales were stirring all of us. Louisa, from Nebraska, said, "It was never a question *what* to do, but, *which* to do!" Ellen told how her grandfather would take her on the trolley from the middle of Dresden into a deep forest only twenty minutes away. He would lift her up into the crook of a tree and then he would sit below on the ground playing his violin. As he played, she would keep watch for the animals that crept closer to investigate. "Another world, another world!" she said. Then Ellen jumped ahead in years and told of war experiences. She said she used to be frightened to think of them, but she had learned that their power was so great she couldn't deny them. On reflecting, she had begun to remember the good that people had done for each other during those terrible times. She said when she put the two together, the good and the terrible, she felt very close to understanding something "exquisitely peaceful" that she couldn't quite explain, something just out of reach. "It feels like a blessing," she said quietly. Something had pulled Ellen back in to find her way through the horror to the heart. As we sat there in the stillness that followed, I felt this unnamed blessing hovering over us.

The "Reflections" questions are opportunities to brush against some of that peacefulness Ellen felt. It's a time to touch, or stand back from, or even hover above, stories told and untold. On a second visit, something not noticed before may catch your eye. After hearing Ellen's story, I've pictured my grandfather lifting me onto a low branch of a tree and I watch the scene play out before me, as he stands safely by. The longer I stay, the more I see. Unexpectedly, sometimes a veil lifts for us and we find a new dimension.

Through our memories we've traveled through childhood, adolescence, and many of our adult years. How often we hear of life as a "journey"! By this point in *Legacy*, I imagine you can picture yourself moving along the paths of that journey, at times being carried, crawling, wandering, running, stumbling, strolling, dancing. Consider the possibility that as you write in this section, your reflections will become lights along the way, guiding someone, encouraging another. And for you, think how beautiful it has been when you've seen a string of glowing lights reaching toward you from the darkness.

We . . . write to heighten our own awareness of life. We write to taste life twice, in the moment and in retrospection. We write to be able to transcend our life, to reach beyond it . . . to teach ourselves to speak with others, to record the journey into the labyrinth.

—Anaïs Nin, *The Diary of Anaïs Nin,* vol. 5

1   How did (do) you expect your life to be at the age of 60? 70? 80?
    90? 100?

Age puzzles me. I thought it was a quiet time. My seventies were inter-esting, and fairly serene, but my eighties are passionate. I grow more in-tense as I age. To my own surprise I burst out with hot conviction. Only a few years ago I enjoyed my tranquillity; now I am so disturbed by the outer world and by human quality in general that I want to put things right, as though I still owed a debt to life. I must calm down. I am far too frail to indulge in moral fervor.

—Florida Scott-Maxwell, *Measure of My Days*

2   In what ways would you say life today is more satisfying than in
    the days when your parents were your age? In what ways is it less
    satisfying?

Kids today worry about everything; it just breaks my heart.

—Julia Wilkins

3 How do you think life today is harder for children? What do you think they are missing that your generation had?

I bring my own life to throw what light it may on how children can be brought up so that parents and children, together, can weather the roughest seas. —Margaret Mead, *Blackberry Winter*

4 Which changes are for the best in how people approach their lives today regarding relationships and marriage, parenting, education?

—Which changes trouble you?

5 Tell of some opportunities you've been given and tell of some you've had a hand in creating.

Some years are good years and we expand in them; some years are bad ones and the most we can do is to hold our own.

—Elizabeth Coatsworth, *Personal Geography*

What did you learn "the hard way"?

Describe a time when your life took an unpredictable turn.

Remember a time when you demonstrated faith in yourself.

6 Looking back on the years after childhood, what do you now see as a time of daring?

—generosity?

—strength?

—reverence?

—creativity?

—passion?

—growth?

7 Who do you think of when you imagine someone saying to you, "I believe in you."

Recall a time when knowing of this belief has made a difference.

For whom have you tried to fill this role and in what ways?

8 Looking back on your formal education, which were the strongest determinants of who you are today and the life you have led? What have the positive impacts been? What would you have done differently at the elementary, secondary, university level?

9 Why did you choose the jobs you had and how did you get them?

How were they satisfying? What were the conflicts?

Why did you stay? Why did you leave?

What is something you learned from each?

If you could, how would you reconstruct the work of your life?

10 Tell of some times in your life when you felt full of energy and hope.

11 Which have been some of your most romantic times?

Tell about some moments of deep intimacy.

12 When was a time when you felt unexpectedly overcome by love?

13 Tell of some times of sweet fulfillment in your life.

Describe an instance when time seemed to stop and you knew you were part of a moment that held great meaning.

14 What are some of the best ideas you've ever had?

15 Write about some of the ambiguities or contradictions in your life.

16 When have you felt most uncertain?

. . . the record of human behavior, the most fascinating subject of all.
Barbara Tuchman, *Practicing History*

17 Which are the fears you've conquered and how?

What is one of the hardest things you've ever done?

18 What changes have you made reluctantly that turned out to work well for you?

19 What situations still linger that you would gladly and eagerly resolve?

20 Tell of a time when you saw a wrong and felt compelled to right it.

Tell of a time when you held back in the face of an injustice. What stopped you and how would you replay the situation?

21 How did you get beyond some of your biases and prejudices?

How have you lost by having them?

22 What have you fought for in your life?

23 What community of people have you felt deeply connected to?
—In this community, what did you receive and what did you give?

24 When were the times in your life when you felt fully committed to something?

What do you think was the driving force behind those commitments?

What were other possibilities that you may have forsaken? Today, how do you feel about those?

25 Having explored thoughts and feelings about many of your memories, what further reflections do you have on the impact of historical, political, and cultural events on your childhood and adolescence?

Write down any further thoughts you have on how your time in history has affected your life as a whole.

26 Throughout *Legacy* you've been giving your reader a sense of place about where you have lived. Take this opportunity to give further reflections on how you were shaped by the landscapes and their climates.

27 Which acts of community giving have been the most satisfying? In what ways? How are you involved in your community today?

28 What are the practical life coping skills you've developed over the years?

Which are the most important?

29 Tell about a friend from each stage of your life, letting us know why you think of that person as your friend.

30 Who are the friends of the past you've kept in touch with and where are they today?

. . . since I passed the age of fifty, I have taken to looking back on my life as a whole more. I have looked through old letters and dug out old photographs. I have gone through twenty years' worth of home movies. I have thought about the people I have known and the things that have happened that have, for better or worse, left the deepest mark on me.
— Frederick Buechner, *The Sacred Journey*

31 What and who have been the greatest influences on your life and in what ways?

Share how different people have helped bring out parts of your self.

32 What were some times you followed your intuition and what times did you hold back?

33 Write about a lost opportunity.

34 What disadvantages or limitations have you faced in your life, and how have you dealt with them?

35　When was a time your courage sustained you?

Describe some acts of kindness or compassion you've experienced.

Which are the thoughts and memories that bring tears?

Tell about the time in your life that you would consider the end of innocence.

36　Tell of a time when you felt like running away.

37　Tell about the most difficult betrayal of your life. How did you deal with it?

Which reconciliations and acts of forgiveness have meant the most to you?

The scenes come back like separate pictures you find in a forgotten cupboard. . . . The links between them have gone and you're unsure of their order in time. But I notice as I grow older they're becoming clearer and manifest more detail, and relate more one to another.
　　　　　　　　　　　　　—Sylvia Ashton-Warner, *I Passed This Way*

38　Describe some specific moments or signs, no matter how subtle, that show you've been loved in your life.

39　Write about how your interests have enriched your life.

Tell of some times when you know you are tapping into the best parts of yourself.

What talent do you feel you have that you have never developed?

In what ways have you expressed
your creative spirit?

40 Describe a time of adventure.

—a time of confusion.

—a time of gentleness.

—a time of awakening.

41 Tell of a time in your life when you
may have been in the greatest danger.

—What other life-threatening situations have you experienced?

42 What stories of your life would you like someone to know that
shed light on what has meant the most to you?

43 Which of your heroes have stood the test of time?

44 Tell of a past event that still holds untouched areas of pain.

45 Describe, in as much detail as you can, your first trip away from
home.

Recall what you can of the time you moved out of your parents'
home.

*Through learning at my later date things I hadn't known, or had escaped
or possibly feared realizing, about my parents—and myself—I glimpse
our whole family life as if it were freed of that clock time which spaces*

*us apart so inhibitingly, divides young and old, keeps our living
through the same experiences at separate distances. Each of us is moving,
changing, with respect to others. As we discover, we remember; remembering, we discover; and most intensely do we experience this when our separate journeys converge.* —Eudora Welty, *One Writer's Beginnings*

46 How did your view of your mother and father evolve through
the years?

What have you learned about your father and mother that has
surprised or impressed you?

*In the week before her death, I, trying to identify myself to her, said,
"I'm the oldest of your four children."
"The oldest?" she repeated.
"The one who wrote those Quaker stories."
"Oh," said she, "did I get those stories written?"
"Written and published," I said.
"I always wanted to write them, but I married early and wasn't well.
It slipped my mind that I did it. I thought I just dreamed I did it. . . ."*
—Jessamyn West, *The Woman Said Yes*

Recall any of your parents' desires or dreams they may have
spoken of.

47 What stands out in your life as something learned from your

parents?

—What do you think they learned from you?

What of your life today would you like your parents to know?

What are the ways you are like your mother? Your father?

What did your parents give to you that you are thankful for?

In the beginning, one loves one's parents. Later, one judges them. Later still—sometimes—one forgives them.
                    —French aphorism

I have cried rarely in these last twenty years, and three of the times have been over my father.
          —Clark Blaise, *I Had a Father*

48   What do you wish you could have asked your parents?

—Your grandparents?

What do you regret about your relationship with your own parents?

What message would you like to send to your mother? Your father?

Bailey was the greatest person in my world. And the fact that he was my brother was such good fortune that it made me want to live a Christian life just to show God that I was grateful.
          —Maya Angelou, *I Know Why the Caged Bird Sings*

147

49 Tell what it has meant to your life to have a brother or sister. Describe some moments that illustrate how you feel.

In what ways are you close today?

50 How and when has prayer been part of your life?

How have your beliefs changed regarding death and spirituality?

51 Tell what brought you through a time of spiritual crisis.

52 Tell of some griefs in your life and how you weathered them.

Which have been your most difficult losses? What have you found you have gained from them?

53 What events have made you question your values and beliefs?

54 Think of events in your life that would have benefited from a ritual or ceremony. To be meaningful to you, what would that ceremony have been like?

55 Recall when your caring and support helped someone through a difficult time.

56 Was there a time when you've felt close to giving up on life? What led up to it?

—What helped your faith in life revive?

I not only have my secrets, I am my secrets. And you are your secrets. Our secrets are human secrets, and our trusting each other enough to share them with each other has much to do with the secret of what it is to be human. —Frederick Buechner, *Telling Secrets*

57 Tell about a time when you felt hopeless or alone. What helped you through that time?

58 Whom would you trust with your deepest feelings and secrets?

Whom could you always go to for honest answers?

59 Whom and what do you praise today?

60 Write about some places of beauty that you cherish.

Margie and I have long discussions about what keeps people going. We both know it's a combination of God's will and good memories.
—Elaine Rothman, "Keepsakes"

61 What is the luckiest thing that ever happened to you and what is the luckiest thing you ever did?

Tell about a time of contentment.

Recall some moments when you felt nurtured.

62 "All my life I've had a sense that . . ."

63 It's that dark and stormy night. The wind is howling as the rain slams against the windows. Of all the places you've been, describe the place you'd like to be tonight.

64 Write about some moments of your life that have touched your deepest feelings.

65 What are some things you've saved that belonged to someone else? Look at one now. What do you think about and what are you feeling as you touch it?

66 What do you still feel sorry about? What could you do to ease your sorrow?

You may in the privacy of the heart take out the albums of your own life and search it for the people and places you have loved and learned from. . . and for those moments in the past—any of them half forgotten —through which you glimpsed, however dimly and fleetingly, the sacredness of your own journey. —Frederick Buechner, *The Sacred Journey*

67 What have you loved most in your life? Things, places, ideas,
    people—as truly as you can, explore why you've held and been
    held by these loves.

68 As you look back over what you have written, what threads do
    you recognize as running through the whole of your life?

69 Which are some of the mysteries of life that you continue to
    contemplate?

70 If you were to be honored for something in your life, what
    would you want it to be?

71 Imagine planning a gathering to celebrate the life you have lived. Include everything that would make it just the way you would want it to be.

72 What are your basic beliefs about people?

73 In your life so far, which are the sacred moments that come to mind?

74 How have you been blessed?

75 What three statements would tell the most about your philosophy of life?

76 So far, which have been the happiest times of your life?

Sources for Quotations

Angelou, Maya. *I Know Why the Caged Bird Sings.* New York: Viking Press, 1980.

Arlen, Michael J. *Passage to Ararat.* New York: Farrar, Straus and Giroux, 1975.

Ashton-Warner, Sylvia. *I Passed This Way.* New York: Knopf, 1979.

Berry, Wendell. *Standing by Words: Essays.* San Francisco: North Point Press, 1983.

Blaise, Clark. *I Had a Father: A Post-Modern Autobiography.* Reading, Mass.: Addison-Wesley, 1993.

Bogan, Louise. *Journey around My Room: The Autobiography of Louise Bogan: A Mosaic.* Edited by Ruth Limmer. New York: Viking Press, 1980.

Buechner, Frederick. *The Sacred Journey.* New York: Walker and Company, 1985.

————. *Telling Secrets.* San Francisco: Harper San Francisco, 1991.

Chernin, Kim. *In My Mother's House.* New York: Harper and Row, Harper Colophon Books, 1984.

Coatsworth, Elizabeth. *Personal Geography: Almost an Autobiography.* New York: E. P. Dutton, 1976.

Coe, Richard N. *When the Grass Was Taller: Autobiography and the Experience of Childhood.* New Haven: Yale University Press, 1984.

Faulkner, William. *Requiem for a Nun.* New York: Random House, 1951.

Glasgow, Ellen. *The Woman Within.* New York: Harcourt, Brace and Company, 1954.

Jung, C. G. *Memories, Dreams, Reflections.* Recorded and edited by Aniela Jaffé. Translated from the German by Richard and Clara Winston. New York: Random House, 1961.

Kincaid, Jamaica. *Annie John*. New York: New American Library, 1985.

Kort, Ellen. "Advice to Beginners." In *If I Had My Life to Live Over I Would Pick More Daisies,* edited by Sandra Haldeman Martz. Watsonville, Calif.: Papier-Mache Press, 1992.

L'Engle, Madeleine. *The Summer of the Great-Grandmother.* New York: Farrar, Straus and Giroux, 1974.

Lewis, C. S. *A Grief Observed*. Greenwich, Conn.: Seabury Press, 1963.

Machado, Antonio. Quoted in *Times Alone: Selected Poems of Antonio Machado,* translated by Robert Bly. Middletown, Conn.: Wesleyan University Press, 1983.

Marin, Peter, and Allan Y. Cohen. *Understanding Drug Use: An Adult's Guide to Drugs and the Young.* New York: Harper and Row, 1971.

Maurois, André. *I Remember, I Remember.* Translated by Denver and Jane Lindley. New York: Harper and Brothers, 1942.

McConkey, James. *Court of Memory*. Lincoln, Mass.: David R. Godine, 1993.

Mead, Margaret. *Blackberry Winter: My Earlier Years.* New York: Morrow, 1972.

Mebane, Mary E. *Mary, Wayfarer*. New York: Viking Press, 1983.

Mencken, H. L. *A Choice of Days: Essays from Happy Days, Newspaper Days, and Heathen Days.* Selected and with an introduction by Edward L. Galligan. New York: Knopf, 1980.

Millay, Edna St. Vincent. "Lament" from *Collected Poems.* New York: Harper, 1956.

Momaday, N. Scott. *The Names: A Memoir.* New York: Harper and Row, 1976.

Morris, Willie. *My Dog Skip*. New York: Random House, 1995.

Neruda, Pablo. *Memoirs*. New York: Farrar, Straus, and Giroux, 1977.

Nin, Anaïs. *The Diary of Anaïs Nin*, vol. 5, 1947–1955. New York: Harcourt Brace Jovanovich, 1974.

Origo, Iris. *Images and Shadows: Part of a Life.* New York: Harcourt Brace Jovanovich, 1971.

Robey, Harriet. *There's a Dance in the Old Dame Yet.* Boston: Little, Brown, 1982.

Rothman, Ellen. "Keepsakes." In *If I Had My Life to Live Over I Would Pick More Daisies,* edited by Sandra Haldeman Martz. Watsonville, Calif.: Papier-Mache Press, 1992.

Sarton, May. Sonnet 2 from "The Autumn Sonnets." New York: W. W. Norton, 1980.

Sartre, Jean-Paul. *The Words.* Translated by Bernard Frechtman. New York: G. Braziller, 1964.

Scott-Maxwell, Florida. *The Measure of My Days.* New York: Knopf, 1968.

Simon, Kate. *Bronx Primitive: Portraits in a Childhood.* New York: Viking Press, 1982.

Stryk, Lucien. "Awakening." In *Collected Poems, 1953–1983.* Athens, Ohio: Swallow Press/Ohio University Press, 1984.

Tuchman, Barbara. *Practicing History: Selected Essays.* New York: Knopf, 1981.

Welty, Eudora. *One Writer's Beginnings.* Cambridge: Harvard University Press, 1984.

West, Jessamyn. *The Woman Said Yes: Encounters with Life and Death.* New York: Harcourt Brace Jovanovich, 1976.

White, E. B. *Letters of E. B. White.* Edited by Dorothy Lobrano Guth. New York: Harper Collins, 1989.

Wolff, Geoffrey. "Minor Lives." In *Telling Lives: The Biographer's Art,* edited by Marc Pachter. New York: Simon and Schuster, 1979.